T0334353

Cambridge Elements

Elements in Music and the City
edited by
Simon McVeigh
University of London
Abigail Wood
University of Haifa

OPERA IN WARSAW

A City of the European Enlightenment

Anna Parkitna
Stony Brook University

CAMBRIDGE
UNIVERSITY PRESS

Shaftesbury Road, Cambridge CB2 8EA, United Kingdom

One Liberty Plaza, 20th Floor, New York, NY 10006, USA

477 Williamstown Road, Port Melbourne, VIC 3207, Australia

314–321, 3rd Floor, Plot 3, Splendor Forum, Jasola District Centre,
New Delhi – 110025, India

103 Penang Road, #05–06/07, Visioncrest Commercial, Singapore 238467

Cambridge University Press is part of Cambridge University Press & Assessment,
a department of the University of Cambridge.

We share the University's mission to contribute to society through the pursuit of
education, learning and research at the highest international levels of excellence.

www.cambridge.org
Information on this title: www.cambridge.org/9781009507806

DOI: 10.1017/9781009323536

When citing this work, please include a reference to the DOI 10.1017/9781009323536

First published 2024

A catalogue record for this publication is available from the British Library

ISBN 978-1-009-50780-6 Hardback
ISBN 978-1-009-32356-7 Paperback
ISSN 2633-3880 (online)
ISSN 2633-3872 (print)

Opera in Warsaw

A City of the European Enlightenment

Elements in Music and the City

DOI: 10.1017/9781009323536
First published online: December 2024

Anna Parkitna
Stony Brook University

Author for correspondence: Anna Parkitna, aparkitna@hotmail.com

Abstract: A microcosm of busy operatic life during the reign of the enlightened King Stanisław August Poniatowski (r. 1764–95), Warsaw reveals complex processes and entanglements affecting dissemination of opera in the late eighteenth century. To the fun-loving city torn by whimsical contradictions, imported as well as domestic opera provided attractive and increasingly accessible urban entertainment, while also serving important utilitarian functions prescribed by local initiatives. Warsaw's participation in transnational circulations of works and performers encompasses both ideological and pragmatic factors that had far-reaching consequences not only for the city itself but also for Europe's shared cultural space.

Keywords: opera, Enlightenment, Warsaw, eighteenth-century music, singers

ISBNs: 9781009507806 (HB), 9781009323567 (PB), 9781009323536 (OC)
ISSNs: 2633-3880 (online), 2633-3872 (print)

Contents

1 Introduction

In the second half of the eighteenth century, operas disseminated more broadly than ever before. The abandonment of *opera seria*'s signature lavishness: elaborate stage display, astonishing effects, and castratos' vocal pyrotechnics made *opera buffa* suitable for multiple productions – also by secondary theatres – as well as wider circulation, including exportation abroad.[1] Demand for Italian opera eventually became so high that it could only be satisfied through prevalence of mobile singers vying for contracts on a large free market.[2] Over a lesser spatial extent, but likewise in transnational terms, *opéra-comique* found appreciation outside its homeland among educated elites to whom literary merits of stage works in the lingua franca appeared as a paragon of refined taste.[3] The Singspiel became subject to expansionist ambitions reaching beyond an established, densely interconnected theatrical space in the wake of rapidly advancing German theatre.[4] All these operatic genres found their way to Warsaw, the capital city of the Commonwealth of Poland and Lithuania (1569–1795), during the reign of the enlightened King Stanisław August Poniatowski (r. 1764–95) by means of periodical hire of incoming Italian, French, and German performers.

The welcoming of theatre and opera professionals fit into a wider plan of obtaining foreign specialists so that to boost progression: Warsaw was on a rising trend, despite its slow start in attaining local importance. Having become the site of the royal residence at the turn of the sixteenth and seventeenth centuries, the city reached the status of a residential metropolis, besides that of the political and cultural centre of Poland, only well over a hundred years later.[5] Following long decades of stagnation caused (among other factors) by destructive wars sweeping through Polish territory, the rule of King August III (r. 1733–63), also known as the Elector of Saxony Friedrich August II, coincided with the earliest modernizing initiatives: reformist speculations, urban planning, and utilitarian public institutions. It was not until the reign of King Poniatowski encompassing the most mature decades of Polish *Oświecenie* ('Enlightenment'), however, that Warsaw went through a metamorphosis as a reform hub. Along with the actions of the open-minded monarch striving to overcome Poland's prolonged sociocultural, political, and economic crisis, it became livelier and more exposed to extraneous innovations. An influx of newcomers, among them foreign burghers attracted by employment opportunities, contributed to the growth of the urban area and population, which reached

---

[1] Piperno, 'Opera Production', pp. 67–73.   [2] Rosselli, *Singers of Italian Opera*, pp. 79–90.
[3] Pendle, 'Opéra-Comique as Literature', pp. 229–30.
[4] The most desired, although not easily attainable, directions of this expansion were Paris and London. *Theater-Kalender* 10 (1784), 193; [Müller], *Beyträge zur Lebensgeschichte*, p. 32.
[5] For a concise early history of Warsaw, see Bogucka, 'Between Capital', pp. 198–216.

about 120,000 inhabitants towards the end of the Stanislavian period, thereby placing Warsaw among comparably large European cities.[6]

Carrying moralistic or otherwise instructional overtones, operas presented by the foreign performers served to bolster a special educational mission of a newly established public theatre (1765) prescribed by King Poniatowski at the outset of his propagandist reformist actions. While promoting a sociocultural revival through performances of both spoken drama and opera, the king fostered the Enlightenment conviction that the arts closely coexisted with political, economic, intellectual, and technological aspects of life, thereby creating civilization.[7] In line with his enlightened, cosmopolitan patriotism, a multidimensional process of self-improvement conducted under royal auspices involved enriching national culture with experiences of other countries.[8] One consequence was that the arrival of operas whose fame transgressed beyond regional and national boundaries conveyed something more profound than straightforward social didacticism: it signalled participation in a shared domain of operatic reception, which may well be deemed a universal domain of the Enlightenment. In grappling with an impasse of ideological ossification among the Polish nobility, repertoire programming had the capacity to not only affect customs and attitudes but also reconfigure reality by situating Warsaw near Enlightenment rationality and creativity.

Regardless, opera provided attractive entertainment – an opportunity not to be overlooked by fun-loving inhabitants of Warsaw. In the midst of pervasive among moneyed nobility habits of gambling, debauchery, and luxury – more unbridled than elsewhere, according to foreign visitors – operagoing appeared an innocent, if not constructive, pastime. Still, it fuelled the city's propensity for insouciant amusement that Enlightenment commentators wished to eradicate; as the learned Saxon immigrant Lorenz Christoph Mitzler complained, the Warsaw audience disregarded morally valuable tragedy and bourgeois drama because it 'only wanted to laugh'.[9] Joining in the circulations of comic operas, besides eventually prompting aspirations for a domestic operatic style (since 1778), accomplished a forward-looking goal of installing refined and moralistic, yet commonly accessible and captivating attraction at the centre of urban sociocultural life. In addition, it opened up more space for superficial lifestyles. Both effects were symptomatic of Warsaw's contradictory character: a fast-growing city indulging in overt moral libertinism while coping with a burden of long-standing social inequalities and political turbulences surrounding the three partitions of the Polish-Lithuanian Commonwealth (between Prussia, Austria, and Russia) in 1772, 1793, and 1795.

---

[6] Grochulska, 'Miejsce Warszawy', pp. 109–10.   [7] See Zamoyski, *The Last King*, pp. 239–57.
[8] Butterwick, 'Stanisław August Poniatowski', p. 50.   [9] [Mitzler], *Dritter Brief*, 46.

The ups and downs of King Poniatowski's politics had vast consequences for the intensity of the theatrical reformist fervour, as well as for Warsaw's operatic life. The first two years of the public stage (1765–67) that coincided with the Enlightenment camp's dominance over the political scene were characterized by strict royal supervision and a bold propagandistic agenda. However, this changed in a gloomy political climate caused by rebels of traditionalist nobility (the Radom Confederation, 1767; the Bar Confederation, 1768–72) and the First Partition (1772). The royal patronage ceased in spring 1767, and the public theatre closed for five years in 1769. Soon after its reopening, the king lost the immediate influence over theatrical matters due to the introduction of a monopoly by the diet (the Partition Sejm, 1773–75) but managed to regain control owing to the purchase of the theatrical privilege by his trusted chamberlain François Ryx (1776), and by providing various subventions. The emergence of Polish opera in 1778 was closely related to renewed, although short-lived, reformist actions; the 1780s showed relatively lukewarm engagement with controversial issues. Then, in the wave of patriotic zeal stirred by the parliamentary debates on the Constitution of 3 May 1791 (the Great Sejm, 1788–92), an unparalleled enthusiasm for King Poniatowski's stance inspired a turn towards an overtly political theatre. Once again, this hopeful moment was interrupted by the unfortunate events: Russia's military invasion in May 1792, the rescission of the May Constitution, the seizure of Warsaw by adherents to the anti-reformist Targowica Confederation (September 1792), and, lastly, the Second Partition (1793). Although the public theatre survived the tumults, the king's strategic joining in the Targowica Confederation made his patronage gain ambivalent undertones. The turn of events that brought an end to the Stanislavian theatre in October 1794 was the fall of the Kościuszko Insurrection against the external powers. Preceded by an unsuccessful uprising in Warsaw, it ensued the Third Partition, the dissolution of the Polish-Lithuanian state, and the king's forced abdication (1795).

This case study focusing on Warsaw's idiosyncrasies and transnational entanglements, while also taking into account specificity of the Polish Enlightenment, aligns with the current thinking about eighteenth-century circulation of operas (adjustable rather than fixed works) in terms of universally engaging repertoires disseminating throughout a common cultural sphere in parallel with performers' extensive mobility.[10] Propelled by demand for opera performance, and possible through increased autonomy of performing professionals, dissemination processes as well as the functioning of specialized labour markets were hardly spontaneous. Complexity of the operatic venture, especially when transgressing political and linguistic borders, called for tactical co-operations effectuated within trading

---

[10] Beaurepaire and Wolff, 'Introduction', p. 3; Korneeva, 'Introduction', p. 12.

systems and possibly through channels of noble sociability or diplomatic relations – various networks of theatrical connections and interdependencies which have recently become of special interest for English-language opera studies.[11] Scholars have focused their attention on intermediaries in transnational operatic dissemination, as opposed to fortuitous circulation of artefacts and trends. Thus, leaders of Italian itinerary troupes, besides being instrumental in taking *opera buffa* across the Alps as early as 1745, played a part in spreading particular operas to non-Italian territories of their activities later in the century.[12] A new light was shed on the importance of *Wandertruppen* for bringing the Singspiel to diverse audiences, also at a handful of locations in non-German polities.[13] Moreover, diplomats acted as cultural mediators between distant operatic stages;[14] whereas specialized agents: playwrights, stage performers, and musicians advised those in charge of non-domestic troupes established at various European centres on matters of repertoires and practices.[15] Concurrently, the mapping of networks and migration paths revolves around the significance of authority figures – hosts (and often generous sponsors) of foreign spectacles – for undertaking initiatives. It has been shown that, from the outset, courts in Central Europe launched *opera seria* independently, alongside rulers' pursuit of 'Italianità' inspired by their acquaintance with Italian culture.[16] A decentralized image of the European cultivation of *opéra-comique* emerged through emphasizing viewpoints and intentions of authorities who invited French theatre to cities outside France.[17] Warsaw exemplifies how repertoire importations, besides resulting from existing predilections of the audience, depended on concrete objectives of King Poniatowski and the profit-oriented entrepreneurs, some of whom were experienced heads of mobile troupes.

---

[11] Strohm (ed.), *The Eighteenth-Century Diaspora*; Bucciarelli et al. (eds.), *Italian Opera in Central Europe*, vol. 1; Herr et al. (eds.), *Italian Opera in Central Europe*, vol. 2; Dubowy et al. (eds.), *Italian Opera in Central Europe*, vol. 3; Woodfield, *Performing Operas for Mozart*; Guzy-Pasiak and Markuszewska (eds.), *Music Migration*; Katalinić (ed.), *Music Migrations*; Nieden and Over (eds.), *Musicians' Mobilities*; Beaurepaire et al. (eds.), *Moving Scenes*; Scuderi and Zechner (eds.), *Opera as Institution*; Korneeva (ed.), *Mapping Artistic Networks*; Markovits, *Staging Civilization*; Glatthorn, *Music Theatre and the Holy Roman Empire*. A Germany-based research group utilized, for the first time, a digital tool for visualizing and analysing the early dissemination of *opera buffa* in Europe; see Hoven et al., *Die Opera Buffa*.

[12] Examples include impresarios who worked in Prague; see Niubo, 'Italian Opera in Prague'; Woodfield, *Performing Operas for Mozart*.

[13] Glatthorn, *Music Theatre and the Holy Roman Empire*. The study focuses, nevertheless, on the centrality of the Holy Roman Empire and its ideological implications for German theatrical enterprises.

[14] This was the case in Stockholm whose *opéra-comique* benefitted from a diplomatic contact in France; see Wolff, 'Lyrical Diplomacy'.

[15] A notable instance of such services was the employment of Charles Simon Favart as theatrical advisor to the Viennese court; see Mele, 'The Adaptation of French Performance'.

[16] Dubowy, 'Introduction', p. 2; Strohm, 'The Wanderings of Music', p. 27.

[17] Markovits, *Staging Civilization*.

An opera centre midway between Vienna and Saint Petersburg, the city further demonstrates the role of factors such as geographical proximity and location.

The place of Warsaw on an operatic map of late eighteenth-century Europe gains prominence in view of a comparably large number and variety of foreign works presented at the public theatre.[18] During the period under discussion, Italian operatic seasons predominated, followed by French and German (see Table 1). But it hardly means that opera functioned as a quintessentially cosmopolitan genre, fashionably removed from the local sociopolitical and national concerns.[19] Ergo, this Element adopts a perspective exploring inter-sections between universalist and particularist operatic phenomena. The firm national framework under the rubric of the Polish Enlightenment serves to illuminate circumstances and reverberations surrounding the presence of foreign opera on the Warsaw public stage, as well as to mark distinctive goals of emergent Polish (that is, national) opera. It thereby becomes apparent that eighteenth-century theatre, indeed, was 'a means of expressing and fashioning identities, at once social, political and national'.[20]

2 The Domain of Enlightenment Opera

2.1 A Noisy City

'Indisputably, Paris, London, Naples, and Vienna are the noisiest cities in Europe. I am very much inclined to place Warsaw next to them. Several districts could well compete with the abovementioned capitals,' noted Friedrich Schulz (1762–98), a literary man and a burgher representative from Mitau at Warsaw's Great Sejm (1788–92) that enacted the revolutionary Constitution of 3 May 1791.[21] It was a noise of movement, liveliness, and spontaneity. An extraordinary number of coaches and horseback riders, day and night traversing through the city core: Stare Miasto, Nowe Miasto, and Krakowskie Przedmieście, added to street hubbub and sleep deprivation. The parliamentary sessions occasioned endless sumptuous parties and dinners thrown by powerful noble magnates lobbying for different political purposes. In teeming public places, polite

---

[18] Żórawska-Witkowska, *Muzyka na dworze*, p. 242.

[19] There has been some scepticism about using national musical types as the principal category of historical research, and some scholars have recently put a greater emphasis on cosmopolitan – that is, universalizing – aspects of eighteenth-century operatic life; see Weber, 'Cosmopolitan, National, and Regional Identities'. However, musicologists have also recognized the importance of various Enlightenment formations for the groundbreaking processes behind the emergence of newer national operas, particularly in relation to German opera.

[20] Beaurepaire and Wolff, 'Introduction', p. 3.

[21] 'Unstreitig sind Paris, London, Neapel und Wien die lärmendsten Städte in Europa. Ich bin sehr versucht, Warschau gleich nach ihnen zu nennen. Einige Theile dieser Stadt wetteifern schon mit den vorhin genannten'. [Schulz], *Reise eines Liefländers*, vol. 1, p. 127.

Table 1 Operatic enterprises at the Warsaw public theatre

Season	Italian Opera	French Opera	German Opera	Polish Opera
1765–66	Carlo Tomatis (beg. Aug. 1765)	Carlo Tomatis		
1766–67				
1767–68		Jossé Rousselois		
1768–69				
1774–75	Johann Joseph Kurz; August Sułkowski		Johann Joseph Kurz; August Sułkowski	
1775–76	August Sułkowski; Johann Joseph Kurz; François Ryx		August Sułkowski; Johann Joseph Kurz; François Ryx	
1776–77	François Ryx	Hamon & Claude Philippe Saint-Huberty (beg. Sept. 1776)		
1777–78		Hamon		
1778–79		Louis Montbrun (end Sept. 1778)		Louis Montbrun (end Sept. 1778)
1779–80				Michał Bessesti (beg. Sept. 1779)
1780–81	Michał Bessesti; The society of Italian singers			Michał Bessesti; The society of national actors
1781–82	The society of Italian singers (end June 1781)			The society of national actors
1782–83			Bartolomeo Constantini	
1783–84			Jerzy Marcin Lubomirski (end June 1783)	Jerzy Marcin Lubomirski; Wojciech Bogusławski (beg. Sept. 1783)

1784–85	Francesco Zappa & Pierre Gaillard	Bartolomeo Constantini (beg. ?)	Wojciech Bogusławski (end Jan. 1785)
1785–86	Pierre Gaillard (end May 1785); Jerzy Marcin Lubomirski (Sept.–Dec. 1785)		François Ryx (beg. June 1785)
1786–87	François Ryx (beg. Sept. 1786)		
1787–88			
1788–89			
1789–90	Domenico Guardasoni		Wojciech Bogusławski (beg. Feb. 1790)
1790–91			
1791–92			
1792–93	Giuseppe Pellatti		
1793–94	(end May 1793)	Franz Heinrich Bulla (beg. July 1793)	
1794–95			(Oct.–Nov. 1794)

people expressed themselves freely and loudly as no pedantic etiquette prevailed.[22] But it was not only during this momentously hopeful, busy time of the 'dancing Sejm', as dubbed by another outsider, that Warsaw witnessed exhilaration and a myriad of dazzling entertainments.[23] The nobility, constituting about a quarter of the city's population, liked to have fun, and the wealthiest often spent their days in a frivolous manner. Cosmopolitan encounters added to the thrill of the *beau monde*, and vice versa: 'Warsaw became very brilliant during the Carnival,' noted Giacomo Casanova, having established himself a member of the local elite, and hence a participant at 'the great banquets and balls which were given almost every day in one house or another' in autumn 1765.[24] Despite the political misfortunes marking the Stanislavian period, the social life pulsated to the rhythm of masquerades (*reduty*), amateur *théâtres de société*, outdoor fetes, public concerts, visits of touring virtuosos, acrobatic gymnastics shows, cheers in public gardens, and other more or less sophisticated distractions. Dance music accompanying crowded gatherings, night sounds of serenades, and street musicians on the barrel organs likely added to the impression that even during Holy Week the noise of Warsaw's dailiness surpassed that of carnivalesque festivities in other cities.[25]

There was something peculiarly decadent about this persistent commotion, a bacchanal atmosphere of 'la capitale du fameux Païs de Cocagne', as depicted in a contemporaneous account.[26] Libertine attitudes towards temporal pleasures spreading among the upper classes, clergymen included, and rampant divorces bespoke a crisis of traditional morality.[27] Schulz could not help noting with disapproval that Warsaw's extraordinary moral laxity, an odd mixture of immodesty and wildness, went in hand with prodigality and other vices.[28] Overt debauchery spurred age-old deprecation of city life as the antithesis of virtuous countryside, but in view of the political affairs as disastrous as the First Partition, which resulted in the loss of one-third of the country's territory and population, Warsaw's gaiety genuinely upset down-to-earth natives and perplexed visiting foreigners. The poet Julian Ursyn Niemcewicz retrospectively lamented over nobles plunging into enjoyment and luxury, as if oblivious, whereas some intellectuals vented frustration in circulating pamphlets.[29]

---

[22] [Schulz], *Reise eines Liefländers*, vol. 1, pp. 126, 151–2; vol. 2, pp. 180–92, 202–4; vol. 3, p. 78.

[23] Daniel Hailes, a British envoy; Engeström, *Pamiętniki*, p. 95.

[24] Casanova, *History of My Life*, vol. 10, pp. 164, 167.

[25] Magier, *Estetyka miasta*, p. 215; Jan Chrzciciel Albertrandi to Pius Kiciński about his impressions of Stockholm in comparison to Warsaw, Autumn 1789, quoted by Ciesielski (ed.), *Skandynawia w oczach Polaków*, p. 37.

[26] [Essen], 'Correspondence', 51.   [27] Snopek, *Objawienie i Oświecenie*, pp. 210–13.

[28] [Schulz], *Reise eines Liefländers*, vol. 3, pp. 49–50.

[29] Niemcewicz, *Pamiętniki*, vol. 1, p. 69; Woźnowski, *Pamflet obyczajowy*, pp. 101–2.

Indeed, despite an official ban on public festivities due to the political disturbances, one could spend the Carnival of 1771–72 quite pleasantly at balls and comedies regularly given at private residences, and *reduty* attracted crowds when resumed in January 1774. The grand reopening of the public theatre on 30 April 1774 – after a five-year break – with the opera *L'amore artigiano* (Goldoni – Gassmann) gratified prevailing needs while provoking quips against the sway of Warsaw's 'permanent carnival'.[30]

No wonder Stanisław August Poniatowski, concerned with his reputation, restrained from attending the performances for over a year. The ostentatious lack of a royal box in a newly arranged theatrical venue nevertheless served as a camouflage: it was the king who initiated the resumption of the public stage, which he himself established in 1765 as a mission-driven platform for morally elevated opera and drama, as well as a home to steady national theatre promoting literary language in accord with French classicist aesthetics.[31] Towards the end of the Stanislavian era, the foreigner Schulz would be surprised at the constraint to maintain a single place of this sort for pleasant socializing, considering Warsaw's ubiquitous pursuit of merriment.[32] Yet this compromise proved valuable for uniquely concentrating, on a regular basis, a composite audience around the king's cherished project of social renewal and cultural advancement. For the price of a ticket, spectators immersed in theatrical enjoyment deemed more educational than the book and, like law, effective in preventing wrongdoing as its incomparable intensity enabled somewhat imperceptible absorption of didactic content.[33]

Needless to say, opera constituting a crucial element of such 'useful entertainment' fit well with the spirit of the 'noisy city'. That the public theatre devoted to rational and refined precepts of its epoch became attractive enough to compete with the trifling pastimes was to a large extent due to a generally high level of the operatic events. 'Comedies, operas, *reduty* continue to be given. Everybody spends their money enjoying themselves', reported a nobleman about Warsaw's social happenings in January 1766.[34] In one respect opera proved particularly valuable for enlightening minds and enhancing customs: being a musical spectacle consistently in vogue, it outlived its usefulness for opulent representational purposes by typically embellishing festive royal

---

[30] Correspondence from Warsaw in *Courier du Bas-Rhin* (7 March 1772), *Gazette de Cologne* (25 January 1774), and *Gazette des Deux-Ponts* (23 May 1774), quoted by Jackl, 'Teatr stanisławowski', 63, 66, 68.

[31] Jackl, 'Król czy Stackelberg?', 65–87.   [32] [Schulz], *Reise eines Liefländers*, vol. 4, p. 64.

[33] [Krasicki], *Monitor*, no. 27 (1765), 208–9; [Mitzler], *Zweyter Brief*, 21; [Czartoryski], preface to *Panna na wydaniu*, pp. 59–60.

[34] 'Komedie, opery, reduty, bywają. Za pieniądze każdy się weseli'. Jakub Regulski to Marianna Potocka, 29 January 1766, quoted by Kaleta, 'Wzmianki', 157.

anniversaries as well as inaugurating the enterprises (equally involved in spoken drama), and as such it made a potent communicative tool. Operatic life in Stanislavian Warsaw exemplifies how this utilitarian function of precious urban entertainment was implemented through repertoire importations dictated by internal circumstances and tendencies, including ideological ones.

2.2 Inviting Opera

Tellingly, the organizational efforts towards establishing the public theatre concentrated around introduction of *opera buffa* and *opéra-comique*. Although the inauguration on the king's name-day, 8 May 1765, proclaimed royal authority in the undertaking, the two *opéras-comiques* of popular origin that were presented that night (*Les deux chasseurs et la laitière* and *Le peintre amoureux de son modèle*, Anseaume – Duni) sygnaled rupture with the legacy of the previous monarch, August III, who transplanted opulent Metastasian *opere serie* (by his *Kapellmeister* Johann Adolph Hasse) from the electoral court at Dresden, along with a rich ceremonial life.[35] No longer was opera primarily performed to magnify royal splendour and noble identity. Rather, independently of the king's musical tastes, newly installed comic opera – an *opera buffa* company launched in August – offered partaking in a voluntary social event; replacing the exclusivism of courtly self-celebration and allegorical pathos with the accessibility of the public stage showing ordinary characters in everyday situations imparted a more engaging role to the diverse audience while providing references to society at large. This, combined with an unprecedented variety of repertoire partly necessitated by the theatre's mixed organizational model – royal stewardship and profit-oriented private entrepreneurship – opened up vistas for Enlightenment-inspired didacticism stripped of elitism, despite being addressed principally to the nobility who constituted the largest segment of the Warsaw audience. Far from serving simply as a means of control (although, according to a publicistic narrative, theatre-going improved moods and therefore productivity), opera added supplementary undertones to the significance of the preferable types of spoken drama: championing social education and contributing to a process of theatrical democratization, both on stage and in the auditorium. An epoch-making postulate of the principled public theatre, considered by one political writer as particularly desirable for Warsaw's vibrant agglomeration of nobles and passing foreigners, came to fuller fruition with importation of recent comic Italian and French operas tackling social

---

[35] For details on the musical repertoire at August III's Warsaw court theatre: parodies of *opera seria* (1739, 1748), *intermezzi*, and *opere serie* (1754, 1759–1763), see Żórawska-Witkowska, 'Parodies of *Dramma per Musica*', pp. 125–45 and 'Eighteenth-Century Warsaw', pp. 40–4.

problems by not only featuring but even elevating commoners.[36] Since its emergence in 1778, Polish-language opera took these ideas to an extreme through unambiguous moral ennoblement of humble characters.

The novel appeal of comic operas carried no less sweeping implications than their suitability to convey social meanings. By the time *cantanti buffi* gave a first performance in Warsaw – Niccolò Piccinni's *La buona figliuola* to a libretto by Carlo Goldoni – on 7 August 1765, *opera buffa* had already gained the status of the most broadly circulating operatic genre: *buffa* productions began to outnumber those of *opera seria* in the 1750s.[37] Likewise, Warsaw's inauguration of *opéra-comique* coincided with the peak in the activity of French troupes abroad that since the 1740s delineated a broad European dimension for French-language theatrical practice.[38] The hosting of operas representing latest creative innovations (action-packed finales characterizing the librettos by Goldoni) and aesthetic ideals (elegant simplicity of music) while epitomizing current fashionability helped to establish not merely a sharper ideologically but also a more compelling profile of the Warsaw public theatre.

The conceptual pillar of institutional permanence, in turn, facilitated fixed term contracting of specialized foreign performers. Vocal dexterity was an important prerequisite for the idea of comprehensive refinement promoted by Enlightenment intellectuals, as well as a magnet for high-ranking members of the audience, in particular, who had formerly encountered impressive opera. The king insisted upon the tactic of employing the best possible performers, especially for leading roles, believing that the supremacy of beautiful voices guaranteed the Warsaw audience's enchantment and continuous interest – even more so than the presented operas. It was thus mainly on the artistic level that the nascent public stage derived inspiration from the past operatic events of August III. The recruitment of experienced singers by necessity followed the rules of competitive economy shaping mobility of these flexible individuals within expanding opera and theatre markets. By providing otherwise unattainable cultural goods, the hired singers and actor-singers enabled Warsaw's connectivity with a universal cultural sphere. However, despite their emancipation from dependence on noble patronage that the coming of the free opera market granted to the singing profession, they had only a limited influence on the choice of repertoire and assignment of roles, save the sporadically appearing in their signature roles celebrated *opera seria* stars.

Initiatives came from the king's circle and private entrepreneurs – the theatrical 'promoters' – striving to achieve concrete goals, be it sociocultural

---

[36] César F. Pyrrhis de Varille, quoted by Pawłowiczowa, 'Teoria i Krytyka', p. 95.
[37] Piperno, 'Opera Production', p. 67.   [38] Markovits, *Staging Civilization*, pp. 20–1.

enhancement or financial benefit. The importance of non-commercial factors, in particular, refutes the preconception (now well recognized by scholarship) that the main driving force behind eighteenth-century opera dissemination was popular success.[39] All the same, popularity played a part in careful repertoire planning, for which the opening of Warsaw's first ever *opera buffa* season with *La buona figliuola*, a particularly celebrated comic opera at that time (premiered in Rome in 1760), could stand as emblematic. By seeing to it that the ticketed public theatre, besides Enlightenment persuasion, encompassed sharing in reception of universally admired works circulating throughout Europe, the king gave a new and strong impulse to local operatic habits. As expected, the *opera buffa* company with its *prima donna* Caterina Ristorini at the forefront evoked curiosity and adulation. 'I have already seen the Italian opera', reported a noble female in a letter, 'and I very much liked Ristorini in action – what a voice and tones'.[40] First-rate opera fulfilled an important reformist postulate of elevated entertainment that was both decent and captivating. Pleasure for its own sake potentially caused harmful effects, but moralizing theatre deprived of entertaining properties was impotent.[41] No less importantly, enticing voices and repertoires reduced the risk of financial failure.

Operagoing remained pleasurable leisure despite possibly entailing unsettling confrontations with moral issues and social tensions. Warsaw's *beau monde* instantly immersed in the delights of the new attraction. 'We are entertaining ourselves a lot here, and have grown fatigued with the spectacles,' wrote a nobleman of high rank in a private letter dating from early December 1765, meaning extravagant exhaustion among his fun-loving social circles whose main preoccupation now became talking about the ongoing theatrical matters.[42] 'In every house and in any place, one mostly speaks nowadays about the spectacles and the people who make them,' reported a noblewoman around the same time.[43] 'The wild days are over, and it is quiet now, but comedies and operas continue', we learn about the end of the Carnival in 1766 from another correspondence.[44] This attentiveness to what was happening on the public stage did not necessarily translate into every-day

---

[39] Piperno, 'State and Market', p. 140; Markovits, *Staging Civilization*, p. 31.

[40] 'Widziałam już też operę włoską i bardzo mi się podobała akcja Restoryni, a głos, tony'. Urszula Wielopolska to Marianna Potocka, 12 December 1765, quoted by Kaleta, 'Wzmianki', 152.

[41] [Mitzler], *Brief*, 9; [Mitzler], *Zweyter Brief*, 21.

[42] 'On se divertit beaucoup ici, et l'on est las des spectacles'. Wojciech Jakubowski to Jan Klemens Branicki, 4 December 1765, in Jakubowski, *Listy*, p. 75.

[43] 'Teraz najwięcej mowy w każdym domu, na każdym miejscu o spectacle i o tych ludziach, co do tego należą'. Zofia Lubomirska to Marianna Potocka, 5 December 1765, quoted by Kaleta, 'Wzmianki', 151.

[44] 'Tu się ty szalony dni tyż skończyły, teraz czycho, ale komedie i opery są'. Madame de Gibbes to Marianna Potocka, 20 February 1766, quoted by Kaleta, 'Wzmianki', 161.

attendance due to the multitude of other – more exclusive – social amusements;[45] hence the theatre's three consecutive venues were typically filled to their capacity only during festive celebrations. Nevertheless, the bustle of penitential Advent and Lent, during which the spectacles continued as usual (except for a two-week break before Easter and next season's opening), exposed plainly a favourable outcome of King Poniatowski's theatrical endeavours: opera becoming a crucial part of intense urban social life.

2.3 Joining in Operatic Circulations

A quarter-century of theatrical seasons (1765–69, 1774–78, 1779–94) saw a considerable diversity of operatic offerings. The king envisioned a flourish of splendid performances regardless of whether relying on repertoire importations, as opposed to commissioning from internationally renowned composers of Italian opera (the musical mainstream at that time), would bestow on the Warsaw theatre a secondary status on a pan-European scale. Primarily concerned with impressing his own subjects, he anticipated that craving for novelty would be satisfied by operas new to the locale as long as premieres occur frequently enough. To the first entrepreneur of the public stage, Carlo Tomatis, this meant a contractual stipulation that he produced one Italian opera per month.[46] Such intensity was significant considering that the busiest period for the court theatre of August III featured ten *opere serie* in a span of four years (1759–63).

The impetus coming from the reformist policy further relied on behind-the-scenes practices governing transnational theatre and opera business. By fostering an impresarial type of royally subsidized theatre and contracted employment, Warsaw made an inviting destination for mobile theatre professionals. In this production system, the entrepreneur taking care of financial and organizational affairs (sometimes encompassing more than one troupe) might share features with the Italian *impresario* as he assembled performers and a repertoire seasonally while subordinating to some extent to authoritative impositions.[47] He was usually a local: a prominent noble (Prince August Sułkowski; Prince Jerzy Marcin Lubomirski), a prosperous trader descending from a Polonized burgher family (Michał Bessesti; Giuseppe Pellatti), or the public theatre's ex-performer settling down in Warsaw while taking on the entrepreneurial profession (Louis Montbrun; Bartolomeo Constantini; Pierre Gaillard). Less often, he was an incoming enterprising manager of a troupe, with a contingent of professional contacts (including some long-time singing employees), theatrical equipment,

---

[45] [Schulz], *Reise eines Liefländers*, vol. 3, p. 4.

[46] Contract of Carlo Tomatis and Kazimierz Czempiński, 3 December 1764, Warsaw, AGAD, AJP, 444; see in Wierzbicka, *Źródła do historii teatru*, vol. I, pp. 6–9.

[47] Rosselli, *The Opera Industry*, pp. 5, 82–7.

and a recyclable musical repertoire (Johann Joseph Kurz; Hamon; Domenico Guardasoni; Franz Heinrich Bulla). Independently of their backgrounds, the entrepreneurs of foreign opera typically secured ventures lasting up to two seasons.

Amid various entrepreneurial fluctuations, the royal patronage continued to affect Warsaw's connectivity with European opera. It began with the rental and renovation of the August III's *Operalnia* – the opera house built in 1748 in vicinity of the Saxon Palace – by the royal court. King Poniatowski supervised the public stage, either directly or indirectly, with the exception of only two instances: his retreat during the turbulent seasons preceding the First Partition (1767–69) and the bestowal of a privilege *exclusionis* to Prince August Sułkowski in June 1774. He surmounted the latter obstacle, stemming from the unfavourable post-partition climate, by having his trusted courtier and one of Sułkowski's financial partners, François Ryx, acquire the monopoly (in October 1776) and act on his behalf in return of subsidies and compensations. The entrepreneurs who rented the theatrical rights from Ryx could likewise count on casual donations. The inaugural two seasons (1765–67) characterized by overriding royal control, going as far as ultimate approval of repertoires, indicate that coalescence of trading methods and social relations behind fulfilling the king's propagandistic theatrical aims was not only convenient but perhaps even indispensable for joining in operatic circulations on the threshold of the public stage. Personal recommendations of the king's brother residing in Vienna as the Austrian army general, Prince Andrzej Poniatowski, led to the hire of Tomatis along with some of the Viennese impressive *buffi*, whose contracting (by means of personal negotiations in Venice and correspondence) remained the greatest challenge on the part of the entrepreneur equipped with subventions and even a theatre building.[48] More assistance came from the king's Parisian confidante Madame Marie Thérèse Geoffrin, although her intermediary in assembling French performers under directorship of the actor Louis François Villiers proved ill-fated inasmuch as the troupe consisting of aspiring amateurs did not live up to expectations and was disbanded prematurely.[49] Yet, without this backing, the recruitment mission of Tomatis's co-investor, Kazimierz Czempiński, would have been doomed to immediate failure due to a mercantilist policy that banned French actors from leaving Paris for jobs abroad.[50] It came in handy that the royal court took the initiative in finalizing direct negotiations with the leading member of a French troupe recently released from Vienna, Jossé Rousselois, a couple of months into the public theatre's opening.[51]

[48] Wierzbicka, *Życie teatralne w Warszawie*, p. 19; Bernacki, *Teatr, dramat i muzyka*, vol. 2, p. 380.
[49] Klimowicz, *Początki teatru*, pp. 22–3.   [50] Markovits, *Staging Civilization*, pp. 63–8.
[51] Wierzbicka-Michalska, *Aktorzy cudzoziemscy*, pp. 45–7.

These centralized actions towards turning Warsaw into a vibrant theatrical and operatic city, one remedy for the country's compound crisis, have been often associated with straightforward notions of 'westernization', or 'Europeanization'.[52] The public theatre's utility as a major channel of modernizing ideals is, however, a far more complex issue. In the first place, Italian opera had been rooted in Warsaw following its arrival at the royal court as early as in 1628, the event that foreshadowed lasting, although not uninterrupted, adoration by Polish elites.[53] Noble residencies across the country had already fostered vogue for operatic activities along the lines of Warsaw's splendid royal spectacles during the era of the two Wettin kings (1697–1763), August II and August III. A striking example of operatic infiltrations can be found in the inclusion of a 'sung *intermezzo* in an Italian style' between acts of a religious drama staged by a Jesuit school theatre in 1763.[54] Furthermore, Poland had long cherished its cultural, religious, and political alliance with the Latin world.[55] The operatic importations gratified expectations rather than artificially implanted an unsettled form of leisure. Neither should the process of drawing the troubled country closer to Enlightenment Europe, as virtually every domain of life required refashioning in the mould of rationality and technological advancements, be conflated with attempts to bring about a cultural unification with the 'West', a 'civilizing' effect of Frenchification, and a negation of national heritage. The once-powerful scholarly idea of an 'Europeanizing project' emblematized in Polish-language comedies by a clear-cut contrast between French- and national-style outfits sported by 'progressive' and 'backward' characters, respectively, has now been generally refuted.[56] Polish enlightened thinkers actually condemned unreflective adoption of cosmopolitan superficiality as their ideal was intellectual openness to universalistic values along with simultaneous perpetuation of uncorrupted traditional customs and national ethos.[57]

Leaving aside the elevated ideas and concomitant clichés that come with the concept of 'educational theatre', the sociability surrounding the Warsaw public stage abounded with moral laxity. The incongruity between the moralizing repertoires and omnipresent libertine conduct sometimes manifesting itself in ostentatious behaviour – such as throwing sacks of gold onto the stage during appearances of admired females – coexisted along with the theatre's enlightening mission.[58] Johann Heine, an agent in the pay of the pretender to the Polish throne Prince

---

[52] See, for example, Gordon and Furbank, *Marie Madeleine Jodin*, p. 36.
[53] Targosz-Kretowa, *Teatr dworski*, pp. 64–6.   [54] Jackl, 'Teatr i życie teatralne', p. 446.
[55] Davies, *Heart of Europe*, p. 343.
[56] The idea was put forward in Raszewski, *Staroświecczyzna*, pp. 295–309.
[57] Kostkiewiczowa, *Polski wiek świateł*, pp. 37–68.   [58] Niemcewicz, *Pamiętniki*, vol. 1, p. 71.

Francis Xavier of Saxony, found Tomatis's *buffi* 'comical and unquestionably good', thereby agreeing with the majority of attendees to the public spectacles regularly frequented by the king, while he also thought 'Sodom' an adequate hyperbole for depicting the life of that theatre and the royal court.[59] Indeed, the king's many sexual liaisons, also with female performers (e.g., the *seria* singer Caterina Bonafini sojourning in 1776 and 1782), endorsed non-prudishness. During the opening season, a sort of fanaticism about the dancer Caterina Gattai (coincidentally, Tomatis's wife) in rivalry with another lead ballerina Anna Binetti led to a tangle of jealousies culminating in a duel between Casanova and the substantial nobleman Franciszek Ksawery Branicki. A handwritten newspaper announcing the arrival of Italian singers for the 1774–75 season scorned at the Warsaw audience's preference for attractive-looking singers over virtuosic singing as it passed on a rumour – not deprived of a note of disappointment – that the newly hired women possessed mediocre vocal talent.[60] Oddly enough, moreover, in the city infamous for pernicious passion for gambling, betting during the performances was not only allowed (until the mid-1770s) but considered a type of subsidy, possibly inspired by impresarial customs in Italy.[61] The contract of Tomatis, himself a notorious gambler, additionally came with monopoly for masked balls.[62] Some found it unacceptable that, in the midst of political tensions spiralling in the autumn of 1766 into mayhem of the Radom and Bar Confederations (1767–72), one could enter the frivolous *reduty* with their theatre ticket.[63] Contrasts and contradictions pertained to everyday life in 'noisy' Stanislavian Warsaw; though seemingly paradoxically, the king's operatic initiative brought about entertainment that on the idealistic plane challenged these very symptoms of mounting sociocultural problems.

3 Towards Enlightenment: Warsaw and Its Opera Audience

3.1 A City of Contrasts

Official estimates dating from 1784 reveal a peculiar disproportion between the sumptuous and the ordinary: a city area embracing 197 streets included a relatively high number of 128 palaces, mostly located in the centre.[64]

---

[59] Klimowicz, *Teatr Narodowy*, pp. 8–9; Klimowicz, *Początki teatru*, p. 59.

[60] A handwritten newspaper from Warsaw, ca. 15 April 1774, quoted by Jackl, 'Teatr i życie teatralne', pp. 501–2.

[61] Wraxall, *Memoirs of the Courts*, vol. 2, pp. 107–8; Rosselli, *The Opera Industry*, pp. 28–9, 71.

[62] Contract between Stanisław August Poniatowski and Carlo Tomatis, 13 September 1765, Warsaw, AGAD, AJP, 444, see in Wierzbicka, *Źródła do historii teatru*, vol. I, p. 65; Engeström, *Pamiętniki*, p. 65.

[63] Kaleta, 'Wzmianki', 165.

[64] Kott and Lorentz (eds.), *Warszawa wieku Oświecenia*, p. 327; Berdecka and Turnau, *Życie codzienne*, pp. 19–20.

An indication of a well-off elite, the stately residencies and the opulence surrounding them (often described with astonishment by the foreign travellers) reflect a persistent nationwide state of affairs that withstood eradication. Archaic feudal relations in Poland, whose nobility enjoyed immense autonomy, remained strong and continued to hold back modernization. Although Warsaw's native burghers prevailed in numbers – in 1792, they made up 65 per cent of the population, whereas the nobility constituted approximately 26 per cent, as opposed to 8–12 per cent countrywide – their participation in public life was disproportionate for socioeconomic reasons.[65] Many urban commoners lived in poverty, unable to compete with better qualified craftsmen and enterprising individuals of foreign origin. Restriction of their rights by the nobility's wide prerogatives had the most detrimental effect on independent initiatives and urban development. A far cry from the situation of non-noble middle classes in some Western countries, Polish burghers were prohibited from large-scale activities potentially boosting growth of an independent social layer.[66]

In the absence of a strong burgher class, sharp social inequalities made Warsaw of the Stanislavian age a scene of shocking contrasts. Miserable wooden houses adjoining princely residencies were not a rare sight;[67] Schulz compares the chaotic cityscape with disparities he previously saw only in Saint Petersburg and Naples. Although, as he also notes, newly erected houses had a tasteful and solid look. The main artery, Krakowskie Przedmieście starting at Castle Square in front of the Royal Palace and merging into suburban Nowy Świat, was most representative with its spacious palaces, churches, and many two- to five-story brick dwellings. The streets Senatorska, Miodowa, and Długa in the noisy city core likewise deserved admiration, but the lanes of the constricted Old Town gave a gloomy impression. The majority of streets, muddy and dark at night, were rather unpleasant to the eye, save scattered impressive private houses.[68] To the traveller William Coxe visiting in 1778, Warsaw had 'a melancholy appearance, exhibiting that strong contrast of wealth and poverty, luxury and distress'.[69] Life among beautiful interiors and gardens, quite numerous in Warsaw, offered tasteful delights and comfort comparable with those of Vienna; but in order to find the city pleasing, one had to be entirely unfettered by lack of time and money, observed the philosopher Johann Erich Biester.[70]

---

[65] Bogucka et al., *Dzieje Warszawy,* pp. 283–5. The remaining estates comprised of clergy, soldiers in foreign garrisons, Jews, and vagabonds.

[66] See Kochanowicz, *Backwardness and Modernization*, pp. 935–6.

[67] Jezierski, *Niektóre wyrazy*, p. 251.

[68] [Schulz], *Reise eines Liefländers*, vol. 1, pp. 79, 86–9; vol. 2, p. 117; vol. 4, pp. 60–1.

[69] Coxe, *Travels into Poland*, vol. 2, p. 170.   [70] Biester, 'Einige Briefe', 552–3, 590.

The consequences of Poland's unique sociopolitical structure reached far. It is thus crucial to situate King Poniatowski's operatic endeavours in the context of his restricted royal power, noble culture, and political matters of the 'republic of nobles'. As noted by Schulz, Warsaw's elite, who seasonally relocated to country residencies and often travelled abroad, belonged to the cosmopolitan *beau monde*, except that it displayed no obsequiousness towards monarchy.[71] Manifestations of proud independence from royal authority among the magnates (*magnateria*), the top rank in the Polish nobility, engendered severe challenges in implementing reforms. Unlike in absolutist states, the position of the Polish king, and even his right to the throne, depended on compliance to the sovereign domination of the noble class that had elected him. The system of 'republicanism with a vengeance', as aptly summarized by Richard Butterwick, empowered the nobility to refuse obedience to a nonhereditary ruler, should he happen to display 'disloyalty'.[72] In fact, Warsaw was under the thumb of consecutive Russian ambassadors while Poland-Lithuania remained under the Russian Protectorate. Catherine II tightened this paralysing dependency under the disguise of an alliance by effectively interfering in Polish affairs. With *liberum veto* in force (with only a few limitations), there was no space for imposition of new laws threatening the wide spectrum of well-protected privileges.

Against the political backdrop, the Warsaw public stage appeared all the more a potent propagandistic tool at King Poniatowski's disposal. The ever-present excitement stirred by theatrical and operatic events helped counteract the power relations unfavourable to the king. If his purchase of theatre tickets for members of the court was a way to support the entrepreneurs, complimentary admission for envoys to the Warsaw Sejm in autumn 1766 could be considered a political tactic.[73] Continuity of the theatrical institution that potentially held sway over the public opinion irritated opponents of change, some of them being former supporters of the Saxon kings' detached passivity. The impetus coming from the king's reformist policy was indeed strong.

3.2 The Audience and the Auditorium

The Warsaw audience that mirrored the existing social divisions indicates an ambiguous relationship between opera and operagoers at large. The overall weakness of Polish burghers, resulting in their limited contribution to political and intellectual affairs, does not fit into Jürgen Habermas's association of groundbreaking transformations of the public sphere during the early modern

---

[71] [Schulz], *Reise eines Liefländers*, vol. 2, pp. 174, 176–7.

[72] Butterwick, *Poland's Last King*, p. 16.

[73] Klimowicz, 'Repertuar teatru warszawskiego', 254.

period with the dynamic ascent of the bourgeoisie.[74] The alleged emancipation
of audiences in the age of *opera buffa*, described by Theodor W. Adorno as 'so
far advanced that opera hardly isolated itself from the bourgeoisie', took place
without Warsaw's weighty contribution.[75] For starters, one cannot speak of an
advancing 'pure' bourgeois culture in eighteenth-century Poland.[76] But this is
not to say that urban commoners, ranging from humble craftsmen to rich
patricians, were uninterested in operagoing; the fact that the entrepreneur of
the Italian company in 1785, Jerzy Marcin Lubomirski, offered monthly subscriptions for the gallery and the top open floor called *paradyz* provides one
evidence.[77] Neither were the Warsaw burghers uninvolved in pursuit of greater
civil and political rights, opening ways to dignity and material prosperity.[78] The
problem lay in their restricted capacity to fulfil emancipating ambitions, easy
access to urban leisure activities included, as reflected in the nobility's predom-
inant role in inspiring modernizing processes. Seeing opulence and ennoblement as the only certain paths to social promotion, the wealthy (e.g., bankers)
imitated the nobility in dress and lifestyle, rather than strived to shape
a vigorous, distinct culture of their own.[79] Eager to fit to the high social circles,
aspiring well-off burghers reserved theatre seats in the close proximity of
respectable nobles; the name of the banker Piotr Blank, for example, can be
found among Ryx's subscribers for parterre-level boxes.[80]

The segregation of the audience by social rank reveals typical deficiencies in
the democratization of the public theatre.[81] The introduction of paid admission
sustained the old order whereby the most comfortable, exposed, and expensive
areas in the auditorium were destined for the privileged. The custom of prepaid
seasonal box rentals, which helped the Warsaw entrepreneurs maximize profit,
reinforced insuperable social barriers. Yearly charges for premier boxes of
the second tier amounted roughly to equivalent of two-year earnings of the
average Polish actor, orchestra musician, or craftsman. More affordable options
included short-term or one-night box rentals, as well as subscriptions for the
parterre and the gallery. But to the majority of burghers, regular attendance and
choosing best seats in the auditorium represented unrealistic choice, and even
relatively high prices for single tickets hampered their participation in theatrical
and operatic life. Besides the economic reasons, class prejudice exerted a strong

---

[74] Habermas, *The Structural Transformation*. See counterarguments in Blanning, *The Culture of Power*, p. 12.
[75] Adorno, 'Bourgeois Opera', pp. 19–20.
[76] Bogucka and Samsonowicz, *Dzieje miast*, p. 548.
[77] 'Doniesienie', Warsaw, ISPAN, AMR, 1067 63 (1).
[78] See Murphy, *From Citizens to Subjects*, pp. 25–7.   [79] Tazbir, *Kultura szlachecka*, pp. 47–51.
[80] A list of box subscribers in 1777, Cracow, BJ, 6117 IV.
[81] See Sennett, *The Fall of Public Man*, p. 78.

influence. The theatrical regulations by the general theatre inspector during the initial two years, Count August Moszyński, contained a stipulation forbidding the performers from entering the second-tier boxes at any time on account of their strict allocation to the high nobility.[82] All these limitations show that the audience's patronage still mostly depended on high social status, as opposed to paid admission alone.

The interior of *Operalnia*, the public theatre's first venue in Królewska Street, reflected hierarchical powers even within the top class. In a horseshoe-shaped auditorium for approximately 600 spectators, equipped with four tiers of boxes, the royal box situated on the first floor near a relatively deep stage (having a pair of six wings) was rather moderately decorated with flowery tapestry. On the contrary, the one occupied by the Russian Ambassador Nicholas Repnin ostentatiously stood out with its red tapestry and golden drapery. The primary boxes exhibited individualized looks, and those less prestigious on the parterre level, covered with a rose pattern, appeared more uniform.[83] The circle in front of the stage, whose exclusivity survived through high price tickets, was visibly separated from the rest of the parterre.[84]

Further democratization of theatregoing occurred along with modifications of auditorium space. After the five-year break ending in 1774, the public theatre relocated to Radziwiłł Palace on Krakowskie Przedmieście occupied a hall with three tiers of boxes and capacity of up to 500 seats; here, no measures were taken to segregate audience in the parterre. The king's box – built after the intended hold-up – had a separate entrance and adjoining office space, large enough to fit a mahogany table, a sofa, and four wall mirrors. Tellingly, the maximum capacity of 600 spectators at the third venue, erected by the monopoly holder Ryx on Krasiński Square in 1779, seemed insufficient only about a decade after the inauguration. The reconstruction of the oblong-shaped auditorium in 1791, although profit-driven, evinced egalitarian predilection as the standing parterre with only a few benches at the front was significantly enlarged. The number of boxes decorated with different colours and materials also increased – from sixty to nearly eighty – whereas the stage originally consisting of only a pair of four wings was deepened. On festive nights, the rearranged theatre accommodated up to 1,350 persons: 600 in the parterre, 100 in the gallery, 300 in the *paradyz*, and 325 in the boxes.[85] A simple interior

---

[82] Moszyński, 'Règlement', 1765; Warsaw, AGAD, AJP, 444; see in Wierzbicka, *Źródła do historii teatru*, vol. I, pp. 60–1.

[83] Klimowicz, *Teatr Narodowy*, p. 9; Król-Kaczorowska, *Teatry Warszawy*, pp. 16–7.

[84] As shown by the only surviving playbill from this period (*Natręci*, 26 November 1765, Warsaw, MT).

[85] Król-Kaczorowska, *Teatry Warszawy*, pp. 27–8, 33–6; Raszewski, *Teatr na placu Krasińskich*, pp. 79–104.

design left a positive impression on Schulz; a spacious, beautifully adorned proscenium and varied, functional stage machinery enhanced the theatrical experience.[86]

The parterre was the site of important changes. At first, the lesser nobility avoided mixing with commoners, thereby showing the degree to which the class hierarchy translated into prejudiced behaviour. Despite the king's efforts to encourage more social variety in the standing area by sending there some of his courtiers, during the first season the parterre often remained almost empty.[87] Over time, however, it evolved into the heart of the auditorium where the male part of the audience, including military men, expressed their admiration or critique most explicitly. As we learn from playbill announcements, women with parterre tickets were therefore offered seats in available boxes on the same level at no additional charge.[88] Recurring reminders instructing box subscribers of the third tier to pay extra in case they wished to move to the parterre suggest popularity of the latter. Rowdy nobles in the bustling parterre might well be the reason why the playbills routinely asked 'to show tickets at the entrance in order to avoid quarrels' – some individuals were too proud to approve of the idea of having to pay for royally controlled public spectacles, others felt free to converse loudly for entry price.[89] Prominent box holders might not even bother to purchase tickets each time they showed up.

Steadfast partisans of what the nobility collectively cherished as 'golden freedom' counted among the main addressees of the king's didactic campaign. A closer focus on the noble estate, besides being dictated by its quantitative participation in the theatrical and operatic events, arises from this prescribed role within the public theatre. Among the noble ranks straddling various ethnicities (Polish, Lithuanian, Ruthenian, and more) and levels of wealth, education, or overall sophistication, equality served a mere pretext for claims of privilege. Whereas Warsaw's elite felt utterly at home in the cosmopolitan cultural realm of opera, to the numerous petty nobility (for instance, visitors from the peripheries) theatre still appeared as uncharted terrain that was just opening up through Polish-language performances. Not everybody who fancied themselves an equal member of the 'noble nation' exerted the same power and demonstrated a high degree of insight into the sociopolitical situation; at the same time, effectiveness of the reformist undertakings depended a great deal on whether they could first inspire a uniformity in willingness to revise one's way of thinking.

---

[86] [Schulz], *Reise eines Liefländers*, vol. 4, pp. 65–6.

[87] Klimowicz, *Teatr Narodowy*, pp. 16, 20.

[88] Playbill for *Lucila*, 22 October 1788, Warsaw, AGAD, AJP, 292.

[89] Playbill for *Fałszywe pozory*, 8 September 1787, Warsaw, MT. Klimowicz, *Teatr Narodowy*, pp. 19–20; [Bohomolec], 'Mci Panie Monitor', 800–7.

3.3 The 'School of Morals' and Opera

Teaching moral uprightness was not a goal in its own right with regard to the Warsaw audience, but rather a point of departure for thought-provoking confrontation with alternative outlooks.[90] The propagandist periodical of the king's Enlightenment camp, the twice-weekly *Monitor* (1765–85) initially edited by the prominent literary men Ignacy Krasicki and Franciszek Bohomolec, proclaimed the public theatre as a secular 'school of the world'; this duty surpassed straightforward instruction for one's moral behaviour by inducing spectators to recognize and contemplate present-day dilemmas affecting the surrounding reality.[91] Particularly during the earliest phase of the public stage (1765–67), the king had high hopes of being able to impose a modified worldview on the noble spectators through Polish-language didactic comedies ridiculing defects of this social stratum. The 'three strongest national prejudices', in his own words: aversion to foreigners acquiring Polish nobility, oppression of commoners, and religious intolerance, became the target. The king's compatriots, although 'generally good people', were immersed in ignorance;[92] the majority remained deluded about what he considered the core problem: the incongruity between degenerating Sarmatian culture and contemporary realities.

The traditional noble mentality had been shaped by a sixteenth-century myth whereby Poland-Lithuania's nobility descended from the ancient Sarmatians, who settled tracts of Eastern Europe at the dawn of the Christian era.[93] This presumed ancestry, both delineating a sharp contrast with the domestic commoners and distinguishing the Polish nobles from upper classes elsewhere, had sweeping sociopolitical implications. In the minds of the adherents of Sarmatism, they were the only legitimate constituents of the nation with a moral right to special prerogatives. Nobles of all ranks considered themselves (at least by principle) equal creators and owners of the republican Commonwealth and were proud of wielding direct political authority, subject to strict guardianship.[94] Since the second half of the seventeenth century, however, full-fledged Sarmatism had succumbed to intellectual ossification, and drifted towards conservative traditionalism.[95] Although high-minded in its essence, noble self-governance went astray, thereby putting at risk the

---

[90] Teaching moral conduct was nevertheless an important purpose of Enlightenment opera; see Nedbal, *Morality and Viennese Opera*.

[91] [Krasicki,] *Monitor*, no. 50 (1765), 387; Klimowicz, *Początki teatru*, pp. 143–6.

[92] Geoffrin and Poniatowski, *Correspondance*, p. 144.

[93] The following characterization of Polish Sarmatism is by necessity superficial and incomplete. Controversies around this complex concept involve questions over whether Sarmatism was primary a cultural formation, an ideology, a type of mentality, or a lifestyle.

[94] On the Polish political culture, see: Walicki, *The Enlightenment and the Birth of Modern Nationhood*; Lukowski, *Disorderly Liberty*; Grześkowiak-Krwawicz, *Queen Liberty*.

[95] Pelc, *Barok*, pp. 231–2.

development and sovereignty of the state. The *liberum veto* that came into use revealed unreflective conformism. During the Saxon days, a Sarmatian sense of superiority often took a turn towards narrow-minded megalomania. Egocentric members of contending magnate families augmented possessions and spheres of influence by subordinating lesser – or impoverished – nobles. Preoccupied with protection of individual freedoms as the fundamental guarantee of the existing governmental system, viewed as utterly perfect, the nobility overlooked the increasing incompatibility of Poland's 'extreme form of democracy' (as described by Norman Davies) with the danger of foreign absolutism.[96] The multiple problems, which indeed led to the disappearance of the state in 1795, grew concurrently with omnipresent reluctance to change. As a result, pride in the unique republican system, considered morally superior to European superpower politics and international stratagems, mutated into arrogant disdain towards other countries and foreigners; the mythical lineage diluted responsibility for abuse of serfs inescapably tied to the nobility's land; and, lastly, the fear of destroying the 'flawless' order prompted distrust towards the outside 'other'. The three national sins recognized by the king could well be named xenophobia, exploitation, and fanaticism – traps of the warped concept of liberty understood as the highest value, supplanting rather than guaranteeing other constituents of human happiness.[97] As such, they came under enlightened criticism along with other shameful defects of the lazy mind: negligence, bigotry, litigiousness, imprudence, and superstition.

Early Polish comedies that were specially created under dictation of King Poniatowski's agenda exposed and denounced these shortcomings in the most unambiguous way. Shaped by a top-down scheme whereby characters are constructed around a single trait, either clearly positive or negative, they lacked deepened psychological portrayals. Extreme pragmatism justified oversimplifications, even at the cost of a weakened comic effect.[98] Uncomplicated librettos to the first original Polish operas, also little spontaneous products, still owed much to this formulaic method of weaving utterly immoral figures into the plots so as to highlight the others' virtues – without, however, reproaching specific persons or incorporating elements repudiating national customs and history.

With respect to the latter point, it signals that the public theatre's didactic mission, the epoch-making confrontation of past and present, did not revolve around a clear-cut dichotomy between 'backward' Sarmatism and 'progressive' Enlightenment. Studies discrediting generalizations of this sort underline coexistence of many different – even quite contradictory – intellectual currents and attitudes.[99]

---

[96] Davies, *Heart of Europe*, pp. 296–7.   [97] Grześkowiak-Krwawicz, *Queen Liberty*, p. 86.

[98] Ratajczakowa, *Komedia oświeconych*, p. 68.

[99] See the pioneering study along these lines by Maciejewski, 'Geneza i charakter ideologii republikantów', 45–84.

Traditionalist nobles were often acquainted with the most recent cosmopolitan fashions while indifferent to philosophical debates and sociocultural advancements. Sarmatism itself was diverse and, since the mid eighteenth century, inclined to revision.[100] The reformers showed no intention to replace the old heritage with new models, but rather aimed to assimilate the praiseworthy aspects of native culture, the legacy of the Sarmatian foundations, into the programme of rethinking self-identity and underlining present-day responsibilities.[101] The conscious commitment to continuation and refinement of domestic traditions within the universalistic framework of modernization has been deemed an important, if not a decisive, factor in shaping the particularistic character of Polish eighteenth-century culture.[102]

The specificity of the Polish Enlightenment provides a useful context through which to understand emergent Polish opera: spoken comedy interspersed with sung numbers, whose rustic themes unprecedentedly dignified commoners on stage. Before the public theatre's educative programme somewhat loosened in the 1780s, originally composed operas in the vernacular denounced exploitation of the native peasants by depicting a trenchant contrast between the oppressors and the oppressed. But instead of advocating for immediate abolition of serfdom and the established social order, they attempted to generate a constructive impulse toward overcoming the economic and political stagnation, evident through the cripple of anachronistic policies and the nobility's self-interest. Along with elevating the serfs in a way opposite to the pervading disdain, these operas promoted an image of the humane landowner, that is, actively involved in bettering the fate of his subjects. Young peasants Kasia and Antek in the first Polish opera, *Nędza uszczęśliwiona* (*Misery Made Happy*, 1778; libretto by Wojciech Bogusławski, music by Maciej Kamieński) escape extreme poverty thanks to a master who, having 'learned to love his people', invests the couple with essential goods, thereby enabling their marriage.[103] Hanulka and Antek from *Prostota cnotliwa* (*Virtuous Simplicity*, 1779; libretto by Franciszek Bohomolec, music by Kamieński) find happiness together after the girl escapes advances of an obtrusive clerk thanks to the liberation of her village by a new owner, 'an angel and pure goodness'.[104] Exploring a similarly schematic love story, *Zośka czyli wiejskie zaloty* (*Sophia, or Country Courtship*, 1779; libretto by Stanisław Szymański, music by Kamieński) strikes an ominous note of warning against a revengeful peasant rebellion.[105] One could assess greater

---

[100] See Roszak, *Środowisko intelektualne*, pp. 11–26.
[101] Kostkiewiczowa, *Polski wiek świateł*, pp. 79–89, 404–13.
[102] Parkitny, *Nowoczesność oświecenia*, pp. 104–5.
[103] *Nędza uszczęśliwiona* (Warsaw: Dufour, 1778).
[104] *Prostota cnotliwa* (Warsaw: Drukarnia Nadworna J.K. Mci, 1779).
[105] *Zośka czyli wiejskie zaloty*, 2nd ed. (Warsaw: Dufour, 1784).

significance to the explicit social criticism in *Nędza uszczęśliwiona* than to musical naivety of the arias which, nevertheless, made a reasonable comprom-ise in juxtaposition to the straightforward plot (alas, the other scores have not survived). Folk melodic and rhythmic stylizations, as well as inclusion of popular songs in the later two operas (as we learn from the surviving librettos and descriptions), enhanced the sense of local colour by which exploitations of familiar national elements along with absorbed Italian and French musical idioms gained an entirely unique character. The morality of the main characters shows no ambiguity while their humble social ranks remain unchanged, unlike in the case of only seemingly plebeian sentimental heroines in *opera buffa* (e.g., *La buona figliuola*), or certain fluidity in class divisions characterizing bour-geois drama.[106] *Prostota cnotliwa*, labelled as pastoral opera in the libretto, referred to the topos of unspoiled Arcadia – often present in *opéra-comique* – on the condition that happiness of the villagers living in harmony and devotion to help others derived from their legal status of free people, descendants of the burgher stratum or enfranchised peasants. The crucial feature was the potential to evoke sympathy and pity in the spectator; the young inhabitants of the countryside demonstrate through their virtue that they deserve decent living conditions. What better way to indirectly support the reformist proposals announced in summer 1778, the so-called Zamoyski Code, that concentrated on gradual emancipation of the commoners (eventually rejected by the Sejm of 1780).

The absorption of the operatic genre by the national theatre led to equating significance of originally composed and adapted works in terms of their moral instruction, aesthetics, and entertaining role.[107] Adaptations equally contributing to the growing stock of Polish-language operatic productions typically went through nationalizing modifications because imparting familiar features to persons and customs, besides attracting the audience's attention more than alien prototypes, enabled identification with characters on stage and a better understanding of educational contents.[108] The long-time director of the Polish theatre, Wojciech Bogusławski, applied such nationalizing strategies in intuitive responding to the audience's prevailing expectations. Being mostly committed to popularizing Polish-language opera, he championed adaptations of Warsaw's favourite *opere buffe* in sentimental modes – hence morally valuable – before his last operatic project of the Stanislavian era, *Cud, czyli Krakowiacy i Górale* (*Miracle, or Cracovians and Highlanders*; music by Jan Stefani), turned towards political exhortation. This originally conceived opera, premiered on 1 March 1794 and

---

[106] Castelvecchi, *Sentimental Opera*, pp. 59–60.

[107] Golański, *O wymowie i poezyi*, pp. 447–8.

[108] [Czartoryski], preface to *Panna na wydaniu*, pp. 66, 83–4. For an English translation, see Bilton et al. (eds.), *National Theatre*, p. 195.

immediately received to propel an armed resistance to the disastrous Second Partition of the previous year, highlights a shift towards political involvement initiated during the Great Sejm and reflected in theatrical reviews dwelling on patriotic moods among the spectators.[109] Densely saturated with domestic folk inspirations and enthusiastically associated with the pro-liberal Kościuszko Insurrection (1794), it eventually became a paragon of Polish national opera.[110]

Although the imported operas provided less direct parallels with the circumstances ruling in Warsaw, Enlightenment intellectuals emphasized their utility for concrete moral teachings. A pronounced approbation of opera's moralistic and entertaining properties contributing in equal measure to the elevated profile of the public theatre – next to comedy and tragedy – appeared under the pen of Mitzler, the *Monitor*'s editor (1773–78) of burgher descent. While opera figures less prominently in Stanislavian theatrical debates than drama (unwritten operatic rules materialized, for that matter, alongside discussion on the character and goals of the Polish-language spoken repertoire), Mitzler's distinctive inclination likely derived from his musicological expertise. A disciple of Johann Christoph Gottsched, he promoted rationalistic directives for reformed theatre insofar as he found allegedly trivial opera useful in instilling morality. He specifically praised two *opere buffe* performed on the Warsaw public stage in 1774: *Metilde ritrovata* (also known as *L'incognita perseguitata*; Petrosellini – Anfossi) and *La sposa fedele* (Chiari – Guglielmi).[111] The latter's story of Rosinella and Pasqualino, a couple happily reunited after a series of obstacles, provided an example of faithfulness so utterly disdained by Warsaw's high nobility. The *Monitor*'s co-editor Antoni Tadeusz Michniewski, in an unusual paean to *La sposa fedele*, commended power of the singing voice to stimulate deepened reception of the moralistic message seemingly specifically designed for the Warsaw audience:

> Having returned from the opera *La sposa fedele*, which was performed at the local theatre, I immersed myself in thoughts so deeply, that in sort of entrancement I experienced a strange vision. It seemed to me that a gentle wind lifted me several fathoms above Warsaw, and took inside a building hanging in the air, where I found sundry instruments similar to those used by astronomers to observe the rotation of celestial bodies. I grabbed one and, to my surprise, it let me see everything that was happening in Warsaw's households. Dear Lord! What I saw defies description. First, many men similar to the Marchese portrayed by the singer, their lavish arrays, all the luxury . . . Then I saw ladies not quite as virtuous as Rosinella, adept at tantalizing their adorers with delusive hopes . . . Looking further, I saw many sad husbands, like Pasqualino envious of the manner in which lovers behave towards their wives . . . I entertained myself with this view

---

[109] See van der Meer, *Literary Activities*, pp. 133–4.
[110] Bogusławski, *Dzieje Teatru Narodowego*, pp. 76–7.
[111] [Mitzler], 'O dobrym porządku', 504–6.

for a while, and in the end it seemed to me that on one side I heard Pasqualino sing to the husbands, and on the other Rosinella, with her beautiful voice, as in the theatre, address the wives.[112]

Preoccupation with marital happiness harmonized with Mitzler's broader conception of theatre as a medium for promoting enlightened bourgeois ethos and fulfilment of one's civil duties while denouncing anti-social attitudes. The sentimental focus on the private sphere, moreover, valued an individual independently of their position in the social hierarchy determined at birth. With its emphasis on themes of civic virtue, family, and sensibility, *opéra-comique* fit well with this moral thinking; thus the *Journal Littéraire de Varsovie* (1777–78, edited by Deschamps de Saucourt) took the institutional coexistence of French operas and plays for granted. An entire issue of *Monitor* in 1769 was dedicated to the plot of *Le sorcier* (Poinsinet – Philidor) as a pretext to illuminate harmfulness of parental interference in marriage decisions.[113]

The inclusion of non-noble individuals alone did not endow *opera buffa* with a 'bourgeois spirit'.[114] But the class diversity that defines to a large extent the place of comic opera within the Enlightenment's theatrical 'school of the world', teaching rectitude and forethoughtfulness while reflecting real life and thus spotlighting searing social issues, brought with it important implications. In the situation where social tensions exerting a real impact on power of the nobility remained largely dormant, Warsaw's *opera buffa* – whose status of audience's favourite was sometimes surpassed only by *opera seria* – carried an unsettling potential. Amid farcical disguises, deceptions, and confusions, emphatic moralistic messages sneaked into scenes deploring misconduct (e.g., Bartolo's intrigues in Petrosellini and Paisiello's *Il barbiere di Siviglia*). Representations of mental torment – the focal constituents of operas in the sentimental mode – evoked compassion towards virtuous characters, itself a morally positive effect intensified by deliberate compositional techniques (e.g., in Lorenzi and Paisiello's *Nina, o sia La pazza per amore*).[115] An ambience of festive unanimity in finales centered around reconciliation (e.g., in Livigni and Paisiello's *La Frascatana*) likely produced overtones for the audience divided by social rank and political orientation. Lastly, Italian operas focusing on humble lives of burghers (*L'amore artigiano*, Goldoni – Gassmann), tackling cross-class marriage (*Il filosofo di campagna*, Goldoni – Galuppi), and especially those empowering non-nobles, for example, through elegant musical depictions making them indistinguishable from nobles (*Le nozze di Figaro*, Da Ponte – Mozart) introduced uneasy concepts to a traditionalist Sarmatian mindset.

---

[112] [Michniewski], 'Mości Panie Monitor', 121–7.

[113] Issue no. 53 in 1769. The opera's title is not mentioned in the text; see Ozimek, *Udział 'Monitora'*, p. 160.

[114] Dahlhaus, 'The Eighteenth Century', 4.   [115] Castelvecchi, *Sentimental Opera*, pp. 125–87.

Within the local context determining specific reception of the imported works, elements elevating commoners and spotlighting their ordinary situations had a particularly significant meaning. While the original Polish operas based on the rustic themes resonated with the agrarian cult of noble landowners, some *opéras-comiques* exposed the predominantly noble audience to a world of burghers guided by pragmatism and common sense.[116] An adaptation of *Le tonnelier* (Audinot and Quétant – Gossec and others), *Bednarz* (1779) by Jan Baudouin, set the tone for celebrating burgher daily life on stage in the native language, thereby matching Mitzler's postulate of fostering respect for honest physical (or intellectual) work.[117] Baudouin applied remarkable nationalizing methods by relocating the action from a French village to the Warsaw enclave Grzybowo (incidentally, where he actually lived), polonizing the characters to the extent that they obtain more familiar professions (a winemaker changed into a brewer), employing casual language such as Polish proverbs, and making multiple references to customs – and inextricable hardship – of the local burgher community. To complete the task, he replaced some French tunes with songs from domestic urban folklore.[118] The elevation of humble characters reached a new phase through sentimental *opéras-comiques* in a more serious vein resemblant of realistic spoken *drame*; *Lucile* (Marmontel – Grétry) and *Le déserteur* (Sedaine – Monsigny), both adapted into Polish in the 1780s, prioritized moral authority of low-class protagonists over that of nobility at weighty plot moments.[119]

To some audience members, the undermining of noble pride must have been confounding, to say the least; at the same time, however, utilitarian opera did not grow out of extreme ideas. As Mary Hunter observes, there was nothing overtly threatening to the foundations of the existing social hierarchy in the content of Italian comic librettos. Moreover, the virtues highlighted in them (honour, generosity, self-sacrifice), as in *opera seria*, corresponded to the universal code of noble ethics.[120] Supernatural qualities of *opéra-comique* equally served to punish wicked nobles and to reverse effects of magic spells (*Le diable à quatre* by Sedaine and Philidor based on Coffey's *The Devil to Pay*). Some Polish proponents of the Enlightenment, rather than stressing opera's moralistic properties, considered aesthetic upliftment the paramount element of the operatic experience. The editor of the reformist *Magazyn Warszawski* (*The Warsaw Magazine*, 1784–85), for example, shamelessly admitted that Metastasio's beautiful arias, when sung, give soothing pleasure even to those

---

[116] See Charlton, *Popular Opera*, pp. 21–2.   [117] [Mitzler], *Fünfter und letzter Brief*, 71.
[118] Baudouin, *Utwory dramatyczne*, pp. 157–210.
[119] See Doe, *The Comedians of the King*, pp. 56–8.
[120] Hunter, *The Culture of Opera*, pp. 56–70; Hunter, 'Nobility in Mozart's Operas', pp. 177–84.

who 'do not understand a syllable'.[121] Adherents of radical-progressive views were, in fact, sceptical about the public theatre's enlightening mission; the political publicist Franciszek Salezy Jezierski rejected the belief in moralistic effect of comedy on account of its superficiality.[122] Operatic didacticism entailed no revolution – except perhaps in the minds of the king's most fierce objectors, who took the unmistakable criticism of Polish nobles as a serious threat to the old order and a personal offense.[123]

3.4 'Bourgeois Opera' for a Noble Audience

A glimpse at the auditorium through the lenses of contemporaneous sources suggests that the Warsaw audience eagerly succumbed to what Hunter calls the 'sheer entertainment' of *opera buffa*.[124] To many, attending the public theatre gave an occasion for social interactions – especially since lasting operatic conventions somewhat encouraged divided attention – and showing off magnificent looks; it might well provide a mere backdrop for busy sociability. To give one example, Casanova's unacquaintance with the Polish language presented no obstacle to his enjoying premiere of a Polish comedy among distinguished persons invited to the royal box.[125] As we learn from Heine about the beginnings of the public stage, the performances were accompanied by a constant circulation of high-profile spectators between boxes and conversations filled with laughter. The omnipotent Russian Ambassador Repnin applauded performers with an obtrusive *C'est bien, fort bien*! and the king, who himself fostered relaxed but polished etiquette, inspired spontaneity by requesting aria repetitions.[126] Schulz's later account testifies that, particularly during glamorous gala events enhanced by 'the light of a thousand candles', 'the most beautiful, voluptuous, and tasteful ladies in the world' in the primary boxes spread irresistible charm over the parterre. Cavaliers in lavish outfits adorned with silver and gold, carrying sabres studded with brilliants, circled between the boxes as if in dazed delirium.[127] Amid a sensual atmosphere embracing performers on stage, who often became objects of sexual attraction, the parterre rippled with talking, roaring, or whistling, and disruptive incidents necessitated penalties.[128] Many spectators indulged in consumption of drinks, fruit, or ice-cream that were sold during the performances.

---

[121] [Świtkowski], 'Charakter Włochów', 78.   [122] Jezierski, *Niektóre wyrazy*, pp. 102–5.

[123] See Ozimek, *Udział 'Monitora'*, pp. 200–10; Klimowicz, *Początki teatru*, pp. 143–6.

[124] Hunter, *The Culture of Opera*, pp. 27–51.

[125] Casanova, *History of My Life*, vol. 10, p. 175.

[126] Klimowicz, *Teatr Narodowy*, pp. 9, 16–7, 22.

[127] [Schulz], *Reise eines Liefländers*, vol. 3, pp. 4–6.

[128] 'Man plaudert, macht Lärmen, ja man pfeift sogar manchmal ohne Ursache', complained Mitzler; see his *Brief,* 11; 'Obwołanie', 16 July 1775, Warsaw, ISPAN, AMR, 1067 59 (1), in Rulikowski, *Warszawski teatr*, pp. 112–3.

The social mix of the audience, so strongly postulated by Mitzler infatuated with a (still unrealistic) vision of a theatrical venue crowded with urban commoners visiting after a day's work, was not the sole culprit of the noise.[129] A distracting piece of gossip concerning Ryx that completely ruined the gala premiere of Casti and Paisiello's *Il re Teodoro in Venezia* (on 16 January 1785), for example, spread among the nobility's boxes.[130]

The question of to what degree the operatic entertainment was educationally effective remains open. After the first attempts of the national theatre, certain 'reasonable persons' thought the time was not yet ripe for the uncompromising criticism of the existing state of affairs.[131] During the Great Sejm, however, the Warsaw audience revealed a higher consciousness; Schulz describes reactions to political allusions woven into recently premiered Polish-language plays in terms of an ardent patriotic rapture.[132] On the positive side, selective listening that characterized eighteenth-century opera attendees adhering in the first place to their social rituals did not reflect a complete lack of interest in scenic action and music.[133] Palpable in the custom of equipping the boxes with curtains (the royal box at Ryx's venue even had glazed windows), theatrical sociability of the Warsaw nobility involved attentiveness, as indicated by the demand for novelty – premieres, singers, and various embellishments alike.[134] Heine gives us a taste of the atmosphere reigning during an opera premiere (*Il signor dottore*, Goldoni – Fischietti): besides laughter, one heard exuberant clapping arising in various sectors of the auditorium and frequent shouts of *fora!* ('encore!').[135] Indifference to unvarying – thus boring – repetitions of operas that Moszyński (the former Warsaw theatre inspector at that time) witnessed during his journey to Italy was to him equivalent to discreditable superficiality of reception.[136] Neither did language barriers constitute a serious hindrance to comprehending the operatic plots. In fact, Warsaw's *beau monde* enjoyed the reputation of being particularly fluent in French. The majority of educated people also knew German and Italian, which at least allowed them to follow the printed librettos;[137] those accompanying the Italian performances in the years 1765–66, for example, were all monolingual. The alterations visible in the Warsaw librettos for *La buona figliuola*, *Il mercato di Malmantile* (Goldoni – Fischietti), and *Gli uccellatori* (Goldoni – Gassmann) such as aria substitutions and character omissions, sometimes resulting in plot inconsistencies, did not have

---

[129] [Mitzler], 'O dobrym porządku', 507.   [130] [Potocki], *Listy polskie*, vol. 1, pp. 22–3.

[131] Klimowicz, *Teatr Narodowy*, p. 15.   [132] [Schulz], *Reise eines Liefländers*, vol. 3, p. 6.

[133] Weber, 'Did People Listen', 678–91.   [134] This demand is further discussed in Section 5.

[135] Klimowicz, *Początki teatru*, p. 134.   [136] Moszyński, *Dziennik podróży*, p. 200.

[137] Biester, 'Einige Briefe', 591; Magier, *Estetyka miasta*, p. 122.

a negative effect on the reception of Tomatis's Italian company: dramatic integrity gave way to vocal virtuosity as the central element absorbing the audience's attention. Thus, leaving aside the puzzling question of opera's factual moralizing impact, aspects of possibly greater significance should be emphasized.

3.5 Enlightenment through Opera

Along with the public theatre's advocacy for betterment of customs and promotion of modernizing ideas, Polish (or 'national') opera occurred as a unique expression of aspirations awakened during the Stanislavian period.[138] The nation that was perfecting itself strived for cultural advancement through national opera evolving towards an individual style; the makers of Warsaw's national theatre, with Bogusławski at the forefront, aimed at establishing in the long run a strong and distinct operatic tradition. *Nędza uszczęśliwiona* demarcated a symbolic beginning (although it was actually predated by Polish-language operatic undertakings elsewhere):[139] a strand of nascent Polish theatre under Enlightenment auspices whose repertoire formation consisted in gradual accumulation of Polish-language productions. In this, adaptations proved no less useful than original works thanks to the convention of integrating them into native operatic practice purely on the basis of the language of performance. Consideration for linguistic layer served other crucial purposes, counteracting long-time deterioration of the Polish language being the point at issue; as maintained by the *Journal Littéraire de Varsovie*, efforts toward improving the native tongue, propagating its usage, and expanding its range went hand in hand with the moralistic aims of the public stage.[140] 'We should make music in the Polish language because it is an issue of key interest to the Polish people, and their point of honor, to lead their own language to perfection,' argued a musical educator.[141] Having Polish, rather than Italian or French, words set to operatic music – an accomplishment no less momentous than eradication of Latin's supremacy and Baroque macaronisms – opened up an additional channel through which the native language extended its existence into the outer social sphere. Somewhat relegated to a less prominent component, musical

---

[138] The adjectives 'Polish' and 'national' are used interchangeably in accord with the eighteenth-century convention pertaining to opera in the vernacular language.

[139] Polish-language operas by Prince Michał Kazimierz Ogiński were performed at his countryside estate in Słonim (Lithuania) by trained local villagers in the early 1770s. The music has not survived. See Niemcewicz, *Pamiętniki*, vol. 1, p. 114.

[140] See in Bernacki, *Teatr, dramat i muzyka*, vol. 1, pp. 132–3.

[141] '[U] nas w Polskim Języku ma bydź formowana Muzyka, bo Polaków iest istotnym interesem i punktem honoru, swoy własny Język do doskonałości prowadzić'. Sierakowski, *Sztuka muzyki*, vol. 1, p. 151.

invention gained on importance through deriving inspiration from domestic folklore. An essential Enlightenment principle warned against mindless imitation of things foreign, which blurred national distinctiveness;[142] later in the century, appraisal of operatic uniqueness found its way into a publicist narrative going as far as disparaging foreign spectacles strictly on the score of lacking local national characteristics.[143]

Besides spreading cosmopolitan fashions, nevertheless, the imported operas sustained the Warsaw public theatre's idealistic agenda in meaningful ways. The popular acclaim of opera whereby music, vocal execution, and plots became subjects for conversations not only helped to promote a 'good taste', but also made operagoing a crucial factor in continuous resonance of entangled moral and social concerns in the public sphere. Notated arias from operas given at the public theatre circulated for home music-making, and music scores for favourite extracts found usage among noble amateur musicians.[144] In contrast to specifically tailored Polish stage works, however, the incoming operas did not even need to deploy explicit didactic maxims and conclusive morals in order to manifest affiliation with forward-looking socio-intellectual and aesthetic currents: the very presence of *opera buffa* and *opéra-comique* on stage located Warsaw, and by extension Poland-Lithuania, within the Enlightenment world.[145]

Warsaw's integration into the shared cultural domain of opera remained a paramount objective of the reform-minded camp, and especially so before the emergence of Polish opera. Receptive participating in universal operatic culture through works increasingly circulating around Europe was tantamount to fostering the same flourishing cultural achievements as those that had signified marked socio-aesthetic changes elsewhere; in accordance with the goals of the Enlightenment exponents, artistic and scientific innovations that enriched other nations were welcomed in that their effects were universally constructive.[146] The establishment of the Warsaw public theatre – itself an emulation of a positive general phenomenon – thus brought about repertoire strategies transcending glamorous operatic cosmopolitanism of noble elites while forgoing attempts to instigate new influential trends other than those typifying unique national creativity. Consequently, Warsaw's involvement in operatic migrations hardly initiated competition with Europe's prolific operatic cities. The focus on a multilingual

---

[142] See Kostkiewiczowa, *Polski wiek świateł*, pp. 44–5.

[143] [Świtkowski], 'Rozrywki Angielczyków', 178–9. The article concerns performances of Italian opera in London.

[144] Heyking, *Aus Polens und Kurlands*, p. 80; Jackl, 'Litteraria', p. 395.

[145] The presence of the French theatre has likewise been interpreted as affiliation with 'the civilizational project of the *république des lettres*', see Olkusz, 'Poniatowski's National Theatre', p. 82.

[146] Albertrandi, 'Przedmowa', v.

public stage provided a link to the European enlightened community indulging in artful and intellectual pleasures; witnessing acclaimed operas already in circulation, comparable to readership of transnationally disseminating texts, created an immediate sense of belonging.

The initial two seasons (1765–67) characterized by the strict submission to royal control and reformist propaganda demonstrate most evidently the deliberate intention to utilize opera's multifaceted implications for a sociocultural breakthrough. At the public theatre realizing the extensive programme of social education, the selection of repertoire was of pivotal importance. The task fell within the purview of Moszyński, who also had the last word on issues such as castings and decorations. The subordinates Tomatis (the entrepreneur), Villiers, and Rousselois (the successive directors of the French troupes) took limited initiative by compiling lists of operas and plays for ten months in advance, subject to adjustments ('les changements convenables') and the king's ultimate approval.[147] As can be deduced from surviving theatrical correspondence reaching as far back as the months around Poniatowski's coronation, the king specifically prioritized importation of the celebrated *La buona figliuola* along with *Il mercato di Malmantile*, and therefore enquired about singing forces necessary for their production.[148] Doubtless, Tomatis recruitment efforts complied with suitability for the *parti buffe*, *parti serie*, and *parti di mezzo carattere* in the preferable Goldonian operas.[149]

Highest possible artistry and aesthetic novelty became the priorities as the means to build up the theatre's prestige. The thirty-two operatic premieres (in the repertoire reconstructed almost completely until November 1766) themselves made an impressive number.[150] Significantly, operas to the librettos by Carlo Goldoni adhering to the latest aesthetic ideal of *dramma giocoso* (dating from the playwright's second Venetian period, 1748–62) constituted two-thirds

---

[147] Moszyński's instructions for the directors, Warsaw, AGAD, AJP, 444, see in Wierzbicka, *Źródła do historii teatru*, vol. 1, pp. 16–22.

[148] The actor Pietro Mira to the royal secretary Gaetano Ghigiotti, 20 October 1764, Warsaw, AGAD, AG, 451. The letters exchanged between August and November 1764 concerned unrealized plans to arrange an Italian troupe under Mira's directorship; Wierzbicka-Michalska, *Aktorzy cudzoziemscy*, pp. 119–21.

[149] The hitherto unmentioned Italian operas presented in 1765–66 were: *La buona figliuola maritata* (Goldoni – Piccinni), *L'amore in musica* (Goldoni – Boroni), *La contadina in corte* (Tassi – Rust), *La cascina* (Goldoni – Scolari), *Le nozze*, *La calamita de' cuori* (both Goldoni – Galuppi), *La favola de' tre gobbi* (Goldoni – Ciampi), *Il marchese villano* (Chiari – Galuppi), *L'astrologa* (Chiari – Piccinni), and *La cantata e disfida di Don Trastullo* (Jommelli).

[150] The main sources include the following: Warsaw librettos from the years 1765 to 1766; Warsaw, AGAD, AJP, 444 (see Wierzbicka, *Źródła do historii teatru*, vol. 1, pp. 58–9); Bernacki, *Teatr, dramat i muzyka*, vol. 2, pp. 195–323; Klimowicz, 'Repertuar teatru warszawskiego', 241–55 (information from Heine's reports).

of the Italian offerings. Since Goldoni's theatrical reform, works in the sentimental vein were regarded particularly fitting for social instruction.[151] But this desirable feature was surpassed by the operas' masterful innovation. The inaugural *La buona figliuola*, with its three full-length acts, extended finales filled with fast-flowing action, variety of arias, mixture of voice types, and sentimental display of the *mezzi caratteri* was just an overture; within the framework of the Enlightenment theatrical project, the Warsaw audience indeed received a condensed review of Goldoni's operatic pinnacles – fruits of his collaborations with the composers Niccolò Piccinni, Baldassare Galuppi, Vincenzo Ciampi, and Domenico Fischietti. Among them, the vastly admired by European audiences *Il filosofo di campagna* with music by Galuppi (premiered in Venice in 1754) had come as the culmination of the teamwork whose impact on mid-eighteenth-century *opera buffa* (e.g., by means of the drama-oriented ensemble finale) was as significant as that of Goldoni's reformed prose on spoken theatre.[152]

Equally attractive, the French operas were chosen in accordance with the present-day fame of the three most inventive Parisian *opéra-comique* composers before the 1768 debut of André Grétry: Egidio Duni, François-André Danican Philidor, and Pierre-Alexandre Monsigny. The arrival of *Rose et Colas*, Monsigny's most up-to-date stage composition (to a text by Sedaine) and one exceptionally popular throughout the decades to come, deserves a special mention.[153] The range of generic subtypes (parody included) and subject matters (middle-class, pastoral, exotic, supernatural) reflected the variety nurtured by the Comédie-Italienne and Opéra-Comique (which merged with the former in 1762), whereas the works labelled *comédie mêlée d'ariettes* and *opéra-comique*, to a lesser or larger degree departing from the vaudeville tradition, displayed current musical trends. The choice of *Le peintre amoureux de son modèle* for the inauguration of the Warsaw public theatre had symbolic undertones; Duni's first attempt at *opéra-comique*, besides generating rules of incorporating a mixture of pre-existing and newly composed arias, both French and Italianate in style, exerted a wide appeal as a pioneering work of its kind.[154]

Venice and Paris served as points of reference in choosing the Italian and French operas, respectively. Among the earliest Italian comic productions, about half were the same titles as those staged in Vienna in the years 1763–65,

---

[151] See Goehring, 'The Sentimental Muse of Opera Buffa', pp. 116–8.

[152] See Heartz, *From Garrick to Gluck*, pp. 6–17, 38.

[153] The opera adorned the grand royal festivity in the village Młociny near Warsaw, organized on the first anniversary of the Election Sejm on 27 August 1765, and was given at the public theatre in September.

[154] See Heartz, *Music in European Capitals*, pp. 731–5.

that is, during the sojourn of Warsaw's later lead singers, but such parallels often resulted from the wide dissemination of *opera buffa*. Rather, the predominance of works originally premiered at the Venetian Teatro San Moisè coincided with Venice's joining the ranks of the most influential *opera buffa* capitals. Neither did the French operas arrive in Warsaw via Vienna. Despite the extensive competence of Rousselois as a former Viennese actor-singer and *régisseur* (held in esteem by the playwright Charles-Simon Favart who advised Vienna's French theatre), Moszyński did not exclusively depend on his subordinate's experience; even less relevant was Villiers's former Viennese activity as an actor. Tellingly, at least six French operas approved by the theatre inspector had not been at all performed during the comparable Viennese seasons between 1752 and 1765; only one *opéra-comique* by Vienna's house composer Christoph Willibald Gluck – *L'arbre enchanté* (to a libretto by Vadé) – found its way to the Warsaw public stage. The trend was likely reversed only after the end of the royal patronage in March 1767, which gave Rousselois entrepreneurial freedom (among only three known operas given in 1767–69, Gluck's *Le cadi dupé* to a libretto by Lemonnier is indicative in this regard).[155] The king and Moszyński must have relied on some first-hand information – perhaps from a specialized agent – about which comic operas originating from the Parisian theatres made the best choices in terms of artistic value, morality, and commercial potential. For instance, the novelty of recent *L'école de la jeunesse* (Anseaume – Duni, 1765) residing (among other features) in a complex treatment of the vocal ensemble made it an attractive option. Instead of simply following Paris's current premieres, however, the organizers of the Warsaw public stage mostly invested in older works whose attractiveness had been thoroughly verified by Parisian audiences, as exemplified by the vastly successful *Le peintre amoureux de son modèle* (1757), *Le maître en droit* (Lemonnier – Monsigny, 1760), *Le maréchal ferrant* (Quétant – Philidor, 1761), *On ne s'avise jamais de tout* (Sedaine – Monsigny, 1761), *Annette et Lubin* (Favart – Blaise, 1762), and *Les deux chasseurs et la laitière* (Anseaume – Duni, 1763).[156]

All this indicates that Warsaw's incorporation into the shared operatic domain of enlightened ideals and aesthetics, guided by the far-reaching authoritative vision and thereby serving to combat the problems surfacing in social contrasts and prejudices, had a profound significance. The repertoire programming during

---

[155] Reiss, 'Do dziejów teatru', 608. The other two operas performed in the seasons 1767–68 and 1768–69 that can be named are *Tom Jones* (Poinsinet – Philidor) and *Le sorcier* (Poinsinet – Philidor).

[156] The remaining Parisian operas presented during the given period are the following: *La fille mal gardée* (Favart – Duni), *Nicaise* (Vadé – various composers), Soliman II, ou Les trois sultanes (Favart – Gibert), *La Bohémienne* (Favart – various composers), and *Les amours de Bastien et Bastienne* (M-J Favart and Guerville).

the initial years that rested upon the *opere buffe* to the librettos by Goldoni (originating from the playwright's prolific Venetian years) and on the lastingly prominent Parisian *opéras-comiques* was something more than implementation of social criticism, and arguably meant something even more sweeping than association with the Enlightenment community: it induced cultural repositioning of Warsaw towards the very nucleus of groundbreaking operatic invention. It was on this ideologically driven foundation that the intersection of the universalist and particularist (self-redefining and self-enhancing) operatic tendencies occurred.

4 An Opera Centre between Vienna and Saint Petersburg

4.1 A City on the Operatic Map of Europe

Although hardly a touristic destination, Stanislavian Warsaw had a cosmopolitan ambience that affected operatic life. The city hosted a number of high-profile foreigners: diplomats, military men, courtiers, spouses of Polish-born nobles, and long-term visitors, who as a whole comprised a segment of the theatrical audience closely assimilated with the domestic elite. The influx of foreign experts in various branches of craftsmanship, entrepreneurship, art, and science, which was backed by the Enlightenment camp as economically and culturally beneficial, contributed to Warsaw's specific character. Highly specialized persons employed at the royal and magnate courts, mainly of French, Italian, and English origin, easily entered into the top class, whereas non-native craftsmen and merchants, among whom Germans predominated, either got polonized, or cultivated distinctiveness.[157] Maciej Kamieński and Jan Stefani, the immigrant composers of music to the earliest original Polish operas of Slovak and Czech background, respectively, identified themselves with the Polish cultural aspirations. At the same time, cosmopolitan excitement stirred by the presence of internationally recognized performers and stage works – an additional upshot of the busy public theatre – matched the lifestyles of the high social circles more closely than nascent national opera. The success of *La buona figliuola*, evident in ten well-attended repetitions within the first three weeks of the inaugural *opera buffa* season, foreshadowed supremacy of Italian singing which remained the Warsaw audience's favourite until the early decades of the nineteenth century, despite the occurrence of the domestic operatic type.[158]

The German-speaking settlers, reaching according to some estimates as much as one-fifth of the city's population (partially due to intensified migrations in the Saxon era), made up a vibrant, although not homogenous, community with its

---

[157] Zieliński, *Cudzoziemcy w życiu codziennym*, pp. 145, 206–8.
[158] Klimowicz, 'Repertuar teatru warszawskiego,' 242–3; Klimowicz, *Początki teatru*, p. 115.

own taste for dramas and operas in German.[159] As Schulz notes, lives of the German burghers in Warsaw were no different from those led by the Germans in Dresden and Berlin in that they enjoyed the same entertainments.[160] It was mainly with them in mind that the theatre monopoly holder Ryx endorsed the German enterprises managed by Bartolomeo Constantini (1781–83, 1785), Jerzy Marcin Lubomirski (1783), and Franz Heinrich Bulla (1793–94).[161]

The recruitment of German actor-singers also ensued from acknowledging German theatre as a refined and attractive – therefore didactically and commercially useful – species of theatrical creativity, whose speedy progression was an undeniable fact. King Poniatowski paid considerable amount of attention to the German spectacles by gracing them with his presence, contributing financially to expensive opera, and sponsoring deserving actor-singers with money or gifts.[162] Contracting German-language performers acquires a special meaning in view of the tendency, originating in the 1770s, towards standing, as opposed to touring, companies attached to courts and public theatres.[163] It may thus seem ironic that, on the reopening of the Warsaw public stage in April 1774, King Poniatowski entrusted introduction of reformed German theatre's latest achievements to Johann Joseph Kurz, the Viennese creator and impersonator of the character Bernardon in German extemporized comedy, who sought his fortune in Warsaw in the twilight of a long stormy career. Besides a target of Enlightenment's campaign against farce, however, Kurz was former director of the Viennese Kärntnertortheater and an enterprising actor-singer active at various German-speaking locations; his wide professional links proved helpful for garnering members for not only a German, but also *opera buffa* and ballet companies. While epitomizing all that had shaped Vienna's vernacular stages in the recent decades, moreover, Kurz provided a Viennese connection that was deemed particularly precious.

From the outset, Vienna played a significant part in Warsaw's operatic imports. The prestige of theatrical life at the Habsburg capital increased in the mid eighteenth century, and its opera – owing to energetic management of Count Giacomo Durazzo in the years immediately preceding the establishment of the Warsaw public theatre – became impressive enough to compete with that

---

[159] *Mannichfaltigkeiten oder Warschauer Wochenschrift* suggests that the German-speaking population in Warsaw was as large as 20,000 in 1791, see in van der Meer, *Literary Activities*, pp. 129–30.

[160] [Schulz], *Reise eines Liefländers*, vol. 4, p. 17.

[161] Bartolomeo Constantini should not be mistaken for the *Prinzipal* Constantini active in Lüneburg, Hannover, and Kiel at the end of the 1770s (Constantini to Stanisław August Poniatowski, March 1782, Cracow, BCz, 965).

[162] Register of the king's theatrical contributions in 1782, Warsaw, AGAD, ARP, 415.

[163] Williams, *German Actors*, p. 5. For statistics concerning the last quarter of the eighteenth century, see Glatthorn, *Music Theatre and the Holy Roman Empire*, pp. 61–5.

of Paris.[164] The habit of looking to the Viennese opera scene as an example of artistic splendour started with the efforts towards employing Caterina Ristorini, Michele del Zanca, and Giovanni Battista Ristorini who had been spotted there as suitably excellent singers. The arrival of Rousselois, along with Vienna's frontal *opéra-comique* performers: the Clavareau family (Pierre-Augustin, Victoire, Lucie) and Gabriel Soullé, marked the theatrical and operatic path between Vienna and Warsaw ever more clearly. To the entrepreneur Constantini, a search of noteworthy German actor-singers (1781) began with a recruitment mission in Vienna.[165] The successive entrepreneurs kept an eye on Vienna's operatic novelties, both Italian and German. Those whose past experience of enterprising theatrical leaders equipped them with ready stocks of operas (as well as lasting loyalty of some performers) – Kurz, Guardasoni, and Bulla – introduced Viennese works that they had earlier given elsewhere.

As a result of this heightened prominence, Warsaw eventually found itself within the orbit of Viennese operatic premieres. Operas by Antonio Salieri, the Italian music director at the imperial court theatres so closely identified with Vienna that his fellow countrymen suspected his music was under a 'German inspiration', arrived here already in the mid-1770s.[166] The trend – also visible in the presence of works by Salieri's predecessor Florian Leopold Gassmann – culminated, for the first time, in a sumptuous production of Gluck's *Orfeo ed Euridice* (25 November 1776) and again with Mozart's *Die Entführung aus dem Serail* (8 May 1783), likewise given at a royal gala. The premiere of Giovanni Paisiello's *Il re Teodoro in Venezia* (to a libretto by Casti) given by Gaillard in January 1785 – less than five months after the world premiere in Vienna – might exemplify the kind of attentiveness to what was being newly produced and admired on the Viennese stages. During the enterprise of Guardasoni (1789–91), Italian operas originating outside Italy – including no less than five from Vienna – for the first time predominated among the premieres. As former director of a troupe circulating seasonally between Prague and Leipzig (1786–89), the same one that premiered Mozart's *Don Giovanni* and cherished a cultural link with Vienna, Guardasoni brought about recent operas by the Viennese composers Salieri, Wolfgang Amadeus Mozart, and Vicente Martín y Soler; *Axur re d'Ormus* (Da Ponte – Salieri, 1788) turned out to be particularly appealing to the Warsaw audience, followed by *Una cosa rara* (Da Ponte – Martín y Soler, 1786) and *L'arbore di Diana* (Da Ponte – Martín y Soler, 1787), all presented as early as in 1789. The predilection of the entrepreneur Pellatti (1792–93) towards

---

[164] Brown, *Gluck and the French Theatre*, p. 58.

[165] *Litteratur- und Theater-Zeitung* 5, no. 2 (12 January 1782), 25–6.

[166] Rice, *Antonio Salieri*, p. 10.

the Neapolitan *opera buffa* represented by Paisiello, Domenico Cimarosa, and Pietro Alessandro Guglielmi was likely influenced by the current state of operatic life in Vienna, where Leopold II, the successor of Joseph II since February 1790, relegated the home composers to obsolescence through a policy relying on this different type of comic repertoire and *opera seria*.[167] Naples's charmingly simple operas exploiting a sentimental vein, *La pastorella nobile* (Zini – Guglielmi) and *Nina, o sia La pazza per amore* (Lorenzi – Paisiello), had already travelled to Warsaw by way of Guardasoni's later Viennese inspirations.

The connection sustained by the king and the theatre managements also emerged through geographical conditions. Mobile performers and enterprising managers routinely chasing propitious contracts considered Warsaw to be within a relatively convenient travelling distance of Vienna (comparable to, for example, that between Vienna and Berlin). The entrepreneur Guardasoni, whom the Warsaw audience must have remembered as the public theatre's former *primo tenore* (1774–76) recruited by Kurz from Vienna, provides a telling example. Rousselois's successor in fall 1776, the enterprising actor-singer Hamon, offered his services to King Poniatowski – encompassing readiness to stage an impressively large number of *opéras-comiques* – while still holding a post at Vienna (1775), being driven by fear that his unstable venture was at risk of failure, and likely hoping that a move to Warsaw would be relatively smooth.[168] The geographical proximity, a practical factor in lowering travel expenditures covered by the Warsaw entrepreneurs, played a role in organizational decisions. Taking all the factors into consideration, Moszyński viewed Vienna as the most relevant point of reference in calculating costs of potential future enterprises.[169]

Pragmatism prevailed in King Poniatowski's willingness to invite high-profile singers, dancers, and opera composers crossing Polish territory on their journeys between Vienna (or Venice) and Saint Petersburg. What the visits lasting between a few weeks and several months had in common was that they were paid by employees at the court theatre of Catherine II – either newly contracted or recently released therefrom. The celebrated Paisiello (1784), Cimarosa (1787, 1791), and Martín y Soler (1788) were generously rewarded for setting foot at the Polish royal court. Paisiello directed his oratorio *La passione di Gesù Cristo* featuring the acclaimed mezzo soprano Luísa Todi,

---

[167] Rice, 'Leopold II, Mozart, and the Return', pp. 271–7; Rice, *Antonio Salieri*, pp. 493–526.

[168] Hamon to Stanisław August Poniatowski, 12 June 1775 and 'Catalogue des operas bouffons', Warsaw, AGAD, AJP, 445. See in Wierzbicka, *Źródła do historii teatru*, vol. 1, pp. 129–30, 149–51.

[169] 'Memoire Concernant le Theatre', Warsaw, AGAD, AJP, 444. See in Wierzbicka, *Źródła do historii teatru*, vol. 1, pp. 30–8.

who was just moving to Saint Petersburg from Paris, whereas Cimarosa showed off his vocal skills in *La serva padrona* (Federico – Paisiello); both events took place at the Royal Castle.[170] The passing singers enhanced the public theatre's operatic productions. *Opera seria* made a comeback in 1776 – thirteen years after the last Saxon spectacle – thanks to the sojourn of the soprano Caterina Bonafini and the castrato Giuseppe Compagnucci, whose beautiful voices enchanted Warsaw; Bonafini, now on her way back to Italy, stayed again for about a year, under royal patronage, in 1782.[171] The star castrato Luigi Marchesi performed on the Warsaw public stage with the Lubomirski company (1785) in *Giulio Sabino* (Giovannini – Sarti) in which he had sung a month earlier in Vienna, and Anna Pozzi presented her lead role in *La vergine del sole* (Moretti – Cimarosa), originally premiered by her in Saint Petersburg, along with the singers from the Guardasoni troupe (1790). Interestingly, these temporary engagements and guest appearances enabling the performances of *opera seria* on the public stage were first initiated at the time when Vienna lacked serious spectacles; the operatic significance of Saint Petersburg was also on the rise, even more so thanks to the residence of Paisiello as home composer there since 1776. The Warsaw season of 1780–81 became the first to reflect this trend, although by the time *I filosofi immaginari* (with text by Bertati), especially composed for Saint Petersburg, arrived, Paisiello's *La frascatana* (to a libretto by Livigni) and *Le due contesse* (to a libretto by Petrosellini) had already been well known to the audience. The 1784–85 season further witnessed *La serva padrona* and *Il barbiere di Siviglia* (Petrosellini – Paisiello).

The paths of operatic migrations, delineated by pursuit of excellence and practicality alike, define Warsaw's cultural position on the operatic map of late eighteenth-century Europe as peripheral. Complying with the scheme of King Poniatowski, so diametrically different from that of Catherine II fixated on legitimizing Russia's pretentions to Western cultural norms through hire of the celebrated composers and opera commissions, the capital city roughly halfway between Vienna and Saint Petersburg did not generate universally impactful operatic initiatives.[172] Warsaw's operatic exports beyond the Polish-Lithuanian Commonwealth never came off, nor seems it to have been anybody's aspiration, save some composers. Gioacchino Albertini, royal *maître de cha-pelle* (1782–84) in charge of the theatre orchestra, planned a Viennese produc-tion of his opera – probably *Il Don Giovanni,* the first Italian opera to have its world premiere in Stanislavian Warsaw (1780) – but this was blocked by Ryx

[170] Bogusławski, 'Uwagi nad operą *Sługa panią*', p. 308.
[171] [Mitzler], *Fünfter und letzter Brief,* 86.
[172] Porfirieva and Ritzarev, 'The Italian Diaspora', p. 211.

nurturing a personal animosity.[173] When another world premiere of an *opera buffa* took place at the Warsaw public theatre in April 1785, *L'impresario* with music by Albertini's successor Pietro Persichini (to a libretto by Vincenzo Prevato), it was for a one-time benefit night of its commissioner, the *prima donna* in the Gaillard troupe Francesca Buccarelli.[174] The rare instance of opposite direction of repertoire diffusion was the fate of *Der Wunsch mancher Mädchen* by music director in the Constantini troupe Karl Hanke (to a libretto by Ludwig Zehnmark), premiered on 28 December 1781.[175] Having been given under the modified title *Robert und Hannchen* (and with a revised text by Carl Martin Plümicke) in Hamburg – Hanke's next place of employment – in 1786, it reached Frankfurt, Mainz, and Vienna's Kärntnertortheater that same year.[176] Still less was the early Polish opera prone to be exported, although among its few distinguished talents Antonina Miklaszewicz (later known as Campi), who performed jointly with Guardasoni's troupe, ascended to a *prima donna* as Mozart's first Servilia in *La clemenza di Tito*.[177]

But there was also an important, albeit non-mainstream, operatic domain where Warsaw occupied a more prominent position than Europe's chief capitals and the prolific Italian centres: the one of the German Singspiel. Whereas London and Paris remained mostly inaccessible to German opera until the nineteenth-century cult of Mozart took off, Warsaw received a variety of both North German and Viennese Singspiels through hosting the German-language troupes.[178] Unlike in Paris, where the Mozart phenomenon increasingly capturing public's imagination arrived by means of the spoken and printed word rather than performance (resulting in the paradox of many admirers of the composer's genius who hardly experienced his operatic music), Warsaw witnessed some of the earliest productions of *Die Entführung aus dem Serail* (1782) and *Die Zauberflöte* (1791) – in 1783 and 1793, respectively – soon followed by Polish adaptations.[179] The 'belated' diffusion of works by 'undoubtedly one of the greatest of masters' to London, which appeared bewildering in the early nineteenth century, was partially a consequence of not participating in early circulations of German theatre.[180] The territories encompassing the Holy Roman Empire,

---

[173] Wierzbicka-Michalska, *Sześć studiów o teatrze*, pp. 158–9.

[174] Playbill announcement in Bernacki, *Teatr, dramat i muzyka*, vol. 1, p. 276.

[175] 'Journal du théâtre de Varsovie commencé de l'année 1781', Cracow, BJ, 6118 II. See in Bernacki, *Teatr, dramat i muzyka*, vol. 1, p. 224.

[176] For the dates of the Viennese performances, see Link, *The National Court Theatre*, pp. 89–93.

[177] Bernacki, *Teatr, dramat i muzyka*, vol. 2, p. 314.

[178] The division between the North German and Viennese Singspiels is applied in accordance with the classifications established in Bauman, *North German Opera*.

[179] Mongrédien, '*Les Mystères d'Isis*', pp. 195–8.

[180] [Edgcumbe], *Musical Reminiscences*, p. 131.

the Habsburg Empire, and East Prussia, as well as various cities in non-German politics with high percentages of German populations (Copenhagen, Stockholm, Strasbourg, Riga, Reval (Tallinn), and Saint Petersburg), therefore provide the most adequate backdrop for the presence of German-language performers at the Polish capital.

Within these international contexts, Warsaw's operatic undertakings had important reverberations, even though the city was nearly exclusively a receiver, rather than an exporter, of operatic repertoire. The public theatre that often achieved performance standards on a par with Europe's most prestigious opera houses was not only an attractive venue but also made an attractive workplace. With its contingent of proficient and mobile performers, Warsaw woven into nets of similar practices surrounding contracting specialized individuals on free labour markets (Italian, French, and German) and oriented towards satisfying the operagoers became part of the pan-European establishments on the grounds that it opened up possibilities for opera's further flourishing.

4.2 Next Stop: Warsaw

The inspirations coming from Vienna and Saint Petersburg did not place Warsaw within a fixed circuit. The performers were hired from various corners of Europe, whereas the foreign repertoires – affected to a greater degree than during the inaugural two seasons by designs of the profit-oriented successors of Tomatis, as shown by the impact of Guardasoni's inclinations – reflected larger, both universal and local, trends.

Leasing of theatrical rights to specialized mobile managers had many advantages, especially in view of their self-sufficiency in providing a particular type of repertoire. The French entrepreneur Hamon, as he brought with him ten years' experience in enterprising theatrical activities – most recently in Hannover, Brunswick (1774), Hamburg (1774–75), Vienna (1775–76), and again Hamburg (1776) – derived his musical offerings from a set of *opéras-comiques*, listed in the proposal letter to King Poniatowski, that his troupes formerly performed elsewhere.[181] The same is true of Franz Heinrich Bulla, whose choice of *Die Zauberflöte* to be the first musical premiere of the 1793–94 German season must have been motivated by his previous – and positive – experience with staging this opera in Lviv.[182]

The incomers who, by means of their former professional engagements, were also in a position to attract competent troupe members, proved particularly helpful in the case of the French and German enterprises. Ryx made sure to avoid the original mistake of recruiting French actor-singers directly from Paris; in fact, he did

---

[181] *Theater-Kalender* 1 (1775), 178; *Theater-Kalender* 3 (1777), 254.

[182] Bulla, the first *Prinzipal* to have introduced *Die Zauberflöte* to a non-Viennese audience, successfully premiered it in Lviv on 21 September 1792. Got, *Na wyspie Guaxary*, p. 62.

not take any financial responsibility for French spectacles. Due to a shortage of skilled and versatile performers, this was risky business.[183] Hosting a company composed exclusively of masterful professionals would have been asking too much in a city 500 miles away from the French capital, as the *Journal Littéraire de Varsovie* assured.[184] Nevertheless, by closing a deal with Claude Philippe Saint-Huberty, former *régisseur* in Berlin, and Hamon, the monopoly holder invited a respectable troupe for the 1776–77 season: featuring several adept performers for primary roles, and therefore no different from those installed in other European centres.[185] The entrepreneur Montbrun, a Warsaw resident since joining the first French troupe led by Villiers, had no entrepreneurial experience, but nevertheless enough professional contacts to enlarge the troupe taken over from Hamon (in which Madame Hamon secured a central position) with new recruits from Berlin, where Frederick II had just permanently dissolved his French company (1778).[186] The scarcity of singers among the German actor-singers at hand was likewise a problem, which the entrepreneur Sułkowski ineffectively attempted to solve by engaging an existing itinerant troupe.[187] Consequently, his massive efforts to introduce the North German Singspiel in the season of 1775–76 – something that Kurz-Bernardon, a native of Vienna, had not embarked on – mostly failed.[188] Constantini, previously the public theatre's long-time subsidiary dancer, felt obliged to apologise to the Warsaw public for the delay in his hiring arrangements, caused by the general shortage of 'good and excellent' German singers, in the meantime entrusting some vocal parts in actors better predisposed to spoken roles.[189] Such obstacles largely vanished during the German season managed by the proficient *Prinzipal* Bulla, simultaneously director of a German company in Lviv, thanks to flexible relocations of the actor-singers. The valued capacity to assemble a troupe likewise resided in competence to deal with typical seasonal personnel replacements; as exemplified by Hamon, a troupe under a single management, while on the move, was not immune to change. Out of the seven French actor-singers in the 1776–77 season that are known to us by name, only four travelled with Hamon from Hamburg: Rose Gertrude Hamon, Mr. Courcelle, Mr. Victoire, and Pierre Gaillard,

---

[183] See Markovits, *Staging Civilization*, pp. 30–72.

[184] See in Bernacki, *Teatr, dramat i muzyka*, vol. 1, p. 137.

[185] This definition of the 'respectable' French troupe was expressed in the *Journal Littéraire de Varsovie*, see in Bernacki, *Teatr, dramat i muzyka*, vol. 1, p. 143.

[186] Louis Montbrun to Stanisław Lubomirski, 1 May 1778, Warsaw, AGAD, KMWE, 859; *Theater-Kalender* 4 (1778), 230–2.

[187] Negotiations with the *Prinzipale* Wilhelm Schuch and Johann Christian Wäser (1775) ended in debacle. Karl Hertz to Antoni Sułkowski, Warsaw, ISPAN, AMR, 1067 59 (1); see in Rulikowski, *Warszawski teatr*, pp. 122–3, 137–9, 143–5.

[188] Sułkowski only gave *Die Muse* (Schiebeler – Hiller) in May 1775. His affinity for German theatre stemmed from his Saxon upbringing.

[189] Playbill for *Der Freund vom Hause*, 18 August 1781, Warsaw, BN, SD XVIII.4.837.

the future entrepreneur of Warsaw's Italian opera.[190] Guardasoni's Italian company having several skilful singers as its core due to the former activities in Prague and Leipzig: Caterina and Chiara Micelli, Antonio Baglioni, Luigi Bassi, Gaetano Campi, and Giuseppe Lolli, likewise needed new recruits. While loyalty of performers confined to seasonal contracts, the mobile managers invested many efforts into their most inseparable attributes: collections of stage decorations, props, costumes, books, and musical scores. Kurz's own theatrical decorations, although now rather 'worn-out through exploitation in several German locations', as observed by Ryx, accompanied him to Warsaw, and were used along with other ones.[191] Hamon came with a rich assortment of theatrical items; as he declared beforehand, these valuable belongings closely matched specific operas, for which he also possessed musical scores.

What Warsaw had to offer, besides income, was considerable stability of fixed arrangements, even though sometimes interrupted by unexpected circumstances. The complicated paths of Bulla's theatrical ventures, typical for professional undertakings of a dedicated *Prinzipal*, show that a sense of security gained through one- or two-year contracts was a desirable goal. Franz Heinrich Bulla (1754–1819) led a busy lifestyle, equally marked by extraordinary mobility and stubborn pursuit of permanence. Following a debut in Salzburg in the troupe of Karl Wahr, the Prague-born actor started an itinerant troupe that was active in Innsbruck, Augsburg, and Linz. Having met Pasquale Bondini operating in Leipzig and Dresden (1784), he became artistic director of the Prague-based *Bondinische Gesellschaft*, but lost the job after merely three months, thereby becoming relegated to a member of a troupe, run by his former employees, in Pest. Bulla soon re-established himself as a *Prinzipal*, however, and directed Pest's busy theatrical seasons during which he also took his troupe to Kaschau (Košice). In 1789, he moved to Lviv, a city newly acquired by the Habsburgs (after Poland's First Partition), upon request from the Austrian authorities who offered him incentive to settle down there.[192] When he came to Warsaw in 1792 – at first, as artistic director of a short-lived German-language enterprise at Radziwiłł Palace – he must have believed that such a move was worth the effort.

4.3 Operatic Parallels and Variations

Warsaw's Italian operatic repertoire corresponded to current tendencies within the European circulation. The early 1780s witnessed works by a younger generation of *opera buffa* composers, particularly Cimarosa and Paisiello,

[190] [Wittenberg], *Briefe über die Ackermannsche und Hamonsche Schauspieler Gesellschaft*, pp. 45, 49–51, 58–9, 62–3; *Journal Littéraire de Varsovie* (1777–78).
[191] François Ryx, 'Pro Memoria', Cracow, BCz, 965.   [192] Got, *Na wyspie Guaxary*, pp. 31–47.

whereas those by Galuppi, Fischietti, and Gassmann disappeared altogether from the stage. Paisiello's ascent to the composer of most frequently premiered Italian operas dethroned Piccinni, whose operatic titles prevailed in the years 1765–67 and 1774–76. The comic operas by Paisiello, along with those by Cimarosa, made about two-thirds of Pellatti's offerings.

Although an important source of inspiration for some of these operatic imports, Vienna hardly served as a model for strict imitation. As can be deduced from the librettos (no musical scores for Warsaw's foreign operas have survived), the Viennese 1764 versions of the two inaugural operas presented by the Tomatis company in 1765, *La buona figliuola* and *Il mercato di Malmantile*, were by no means replicated. The same holds true for other operas.

A significant example is *Don Giovanni* (Da Ponte – Mozart) introduced by Guardasoni, the opera's commissioner. After Prague (1787), Vienna, and Leipzig (1788), Warsaw saw a new version in 1789;[193] as explained on a playbill, 'the entrepreneur found it necessary to modify some arias in order to make this opera more pleasant'.[194] Perhaps the moderate success of *Don Giovanni* in Vienna the previous year spurred fear of failure. Or maybe the changes visible in the Warsaw libretto served to codify the former Viennese and Leipzig revisions.[195] In any case, Guardasoni strived towards the best possible result, while avoiding dramatic incoherence, by expanding the role of Donna Elvira (first performed in Warsaw by newly hired Maria Antonia Spezioli), applying aria substitutions, and adjusting the libretto to the local circumstances.[196] The latter is most evident in modifications of the famous dinner scene in Act II featuring instrumental quotations from *Una cosa rara*, *Fra i due litiganti il terzo gode* (Goldoni – Sarti), and *Le nozze di Figaro*, originally meant to entertain the Prague audience well acquainted with these operas. Warsaw's operagoers must have recognized the first two extracts: *Una cosa rara* had been recently premiered, and *Fra i due litiganti il terzo gode* revived by Guardasoni. Mozart's 'Non più andrai', however, was not included, perhaps because *Le nozze di Figaro* had still remained in the entrepreneurial plans at that time and there was no use of keeping this element of amusement.[197] All the same,

---

[193] *Il dissoluto punito o sia Il D. Giovanni* (Warsaw: Dufour, 1789).

[194] Playbill announcement of *Don Giovanni* on 14 October 1789 (considered to be the date of the premiere), quoted in Münchheimer, 'Don Juan w Warszawie', 216. The original playbills from this year have long perished; the nineteenth-century source provides otherwise unavailable information. See Bernacki, *Teatr, dramat i muzyka*, vol. 2, pp. 225–6.

[195] Woodfield, *The Vienna* Don Giovanni, p. 116.

[196] Żórawska-Witkowska, 'Wokół polskiej prapremiery', pp. 483–90; Woodfield, *The Vienna* Don Giovanni, pp. 116–24; Woodfield, *Performing Operas for Mozart*, pp. 117–23. There is no Leipzig libretto for the 1788 production of *Don Giovanni*; Woodfield uncovers certain Warsaw-Leipzig parallels on the basis of surviving concert playbills.

[197] The only trace of a premiere of *Le nozze di Figaro* in Warsaw in 1789 is a mention in *Indice de' Teatrali Spettacoli* (1789/90), 231–2. Playbills from that period have not survived.

it is clear that Guardasoni appreciated the improvements especially prepared by Da Ponte and Mozart for Vienna as he enriched the Warsaw production with the lyrical aria 'Mi tradì quell'alma ingrata' of Donna Elvira in hope to suit the taste of the audience.

In the German musical repertoire of the 1781–82 season (which can be reconstructed until the end of 1781), more than half of the offerings overlapped with those in Vienna in the years 1778–79. Constantini, who had no previous experience as an entrepreneur, or even as an actor in a German troupe, perhaps relied on recommendations from his actor-singers, the former employees at the National Singspiel: Franz Joseph Fuchs, Franz Reiner, and Ferdinand Arnold. Regardless, he was not merely recreating Viennese operatic productions; for one thing, a high proportion of operatic adaptations, besides corresponding to the low number and limited impact of original Viennese Singspiels at that time, was typical of German-language repertoires. Rather, Constantini conformed to expectations of his target audience, Warsaw's German-speaking burghers enjoying famous Italian and French operas – whose original versions the local theatregoers had already known – set in a familiar linguistic context. Therefore he chose, for example, *Der Hausfreund*, an adaptation of the *opéra-comique* previously premiered by Hamon *L'ami de la maison* (Marmontel – Grétry). Strikingly, among this German repertoire, only two Viennese Singspiels had originally featured the bass Fuchs in Vienna: *Die schöne Schusterin, oder Die pücefarbenen Schuhe* (Stephanie – Umlauf) and *Die Apotheke* (Engel – Umlauf).

Lack of sources leaves us in the dark about Warsaw versions of the French operas presented by Rousselois, which possibly borne traces of past Viennese modifications (perhaps by Gluck himself) matching the vocal talents of the formerly Viennese actor-singers.[198] Certain vocal deficiencies necessitated simplifications, even as drastic as reduction of ensembles – for example, a trio in *Le maréchal ferrant* – into spoken prose.[199] In any case, musical numbers were typically interchangeable with popular tunes and newly composed arias, thereby bringing to the fore the literary merit of the genre; the violinist in Warsaw's theatre orchestra called Gaitano contributed his own music to *Les amours de Bastien et Bastienne* (the parody of Rousseau's *Le devin du village*), among others.[200] Neither were *opere buffe* thought of as fixed works (as already shown by Warsaw's *Don Giovanni*). Guardasoni's staging of *Le nozze di Figaro*

---

[198] It is probable that *Le diable à quatre* was given to Gluck's revised musical setting of 1759. Since no authorship appears next to the title of this opera in the Warsaw inventories, it may have been wrongly ascribed to Philidor.

[199] Brown, *Gluck and the French Theatre*, pp. 201–6, 405–7.

[200] Klimowicz, 'Repertuar teatru warszawskiego', 250.

in 1791, rather than a revival of Mozart's canonical work, was a new opera by the resident composer Persichini.[201]

The institutional coexistence of opera with spoken plays had interesting consequences that likewise testify to the uniqueness of Warsaw's operatic undertakings. Eighteenth-century audiences were prone to superimpose their memories and impressions of spectacles attended at the same location, irrespective of qualities peculiar to genres and performance languages.[202] The Warsaw audience that was exposed to a broad variety of stage works was kindly reminded of its familiarity with Pierre Beaumarchais's comedy *Le barbier de Séville* (1775) when informed about Lubomirski's second premiere of the 1785–86 season, *Il barbiere di Siviglia*. Recollections of Hamon's spoken spectacles (1777), as well as a Polish adaptation (1779, 1781–83) allowed to anticipate pleasure from Paisiello's opera.[203] The extremity to which mingling of the theatrical events imprinted lasting effects on the spectators is revealed by the playbill for Paisiello's *La serva padrona* inviting to enjoy the performance of Rosa Scannavini, a soprano in the Gaillard company, encompassing an aria in French – the one that Anna Davia de Bernucci (active on the Warsaw public stage in the years 1776–78) used to sing 'in the same opera'.[204] The reference to a former appearance of the Italian singer (most likely, in a French adaptation of Pergolesi's *La serva padrona* given by Hamon) sounds rather confusing;[205] yet, to the Warsaw audience this was a reminder of past delights, reaching as far back as several years, that promised pleasant entertainment.

This further indicates that the connection with the Enlightenment sphere of influence was maintained not only through the operas themselves, but also through the performers, and in particular the most admired Italian singers. Caterina Ristorini, Michele del Zanca, and Giovanni Battista Ristorini recruited by Tomatis had had rich experience performing in Vienna and various Italian cities. This often involved reappearances in the circulating *opere buffe*, sometimes in the same roles. Caterina Ristorini thus had previously performed her Warsaw roles on the stages of Milan (e.g., Roccolina in *Gli uccellatori*), Turin (Dorina in *Le nozze*), Florence (Roccolina, Dorina), and Vienna (e.g., Rosina in *Il signor dottore*). But

---

[201] *Indice de' Teatrali Spettacoli* (1791/92), 176.

[202] Brown, '*Lo specchio francese*', pp. 55–7.

[203] Playbill announcement of *Il barbiere di Siviglia*, 2 October 1785, in Bernacki, *Teatr, dramat i muzyka*, vol. 1, p. 280.

[204] Playbill announcement of *La serva padrona*, 10 April 1785, in Bernacki, *Teatr, dramat i muzyka*, vol. 1, p. 276.

[205] To make things more complicated, we have no other trace of a French adaptation of Pergolesi's intermezzo in Warsaw. We do know, however, that Davia de Bernucci's competence encompassed performing with the French troupes of Hamon and Montbrun.

even more significantly, the three singers provided a direct link with the Goldonian operas fostered by the theatrical management: all had participated in the original Venetian premieres at the Teatro San Moisè.[206] In light of Goldoni's commitment to make his operatic texts support vocal skills of particular singers, Tomatis's employees – besides being adept performers – were perfect impersonators of some famous operatic roles;[207] practical matters, however, decided that Warsaw's *prima buffa* took all primary parts regardless of her former experience. Other far-reaching parallels might result from the entrepreneurs' *modus operandi*; six out of the eight characters in *Don Giovanni* staged by Guardasoni, for example, were in all probability performed by the same individuals as originally in Prague (Bassi – Don Giovanni, Baglioni – Don Ottavio, Giuseppe Lolli – Commendatore and Masetto, Caterina Micelli – Zerlina) and Leipzig (Luigia Prosperi Crespi – Donna Anna).[208]

4.4 Within the Domain of German Opera

German actor-singers possessed a smaller share in the fame surrounding accomplished mobile singers, which was reflected in their comparably modest salaries. They operated within an extensive, albeit culturally restricted, area where German theatre – of which the Singspiel constituted an integral and increasingly important element – found receivers among German-speaking communities.[209] In part it was because mobile theatrical leaders (*Prinzipale*), while delineating the geographical limits of expanding German theatre, felt less constrained by administrative and linguistic boundaries than they did by prejudice and reigning domestic traditions encountered in hitherto unexplored by *Gesellschaften* terrains. The decision of Carl Friedrich Abt to take his troupe, and thus also the North German Singspiel, to The Hague, and further to Leiden and Amsterdam in the years 1772–76, was widely commented as particularly bold.[210] With its large number of German residents, Warsaw had made an accessible and potentially profitable destination for itinerant German-language troupes since at least the 1740s.[211] But the incorporation of a German theatre into the activities of the public stage, whereby it gained a more permanent status, meant that the preferences of the Polish nobility could not easily be ignored.

---

[206] See Wiel, *I teatri musicali*, pp. 207–42. Del Zanca, moreover, was the first Masotto in *Le nozze* premiered in Bologna.

[207] Emery, *Goldoni as Librettist*, pp. 69–70.

[208] This takes account of Woodfield's observation that Caterina Micelli was more likely the first Zerlina, rather than Donna Elvira, see Woodfield, *Performing Operas for Mozart*, pp. 99–103, 116.

[209] Austin Glatthorn has recently proposed the Holy Roman Empire as the main political, cultural, and linguistic framework for the late eighteenth-century domain of German theatre; see Glatthorn, *Music Theatre and the Holy Roman Empire*.

[210] *Theater-Journal für Deutschland* 2 (1777), 127–39.

[211] Wierzbicka-Michalska, *Aktorzy cudzoziemscy*, pp. 26–31.

As it happened, nobles showed generally rather negative attitudes towards the German spectacles. A cabal hatched by certain Polish *Herren* during a German play in October 1775, for example, was so bitter that it prompted two actors to leave Warsaw immediately.[212] The replacement of the German troupe with that of Hamon and Saint-Huberty (1776) ensued in consequence of preferences exhibited by the noble class.[213] This was not due to linguistic obstacles; already the monarchic union with Saxony rendered the knowledge of German fairly common. Nor came ethno-national animosities into play, even if a negative association of German-speaking individuals with the absolutist aggression started to be discernible in the wake of the First Partition (in which Prussia and the Habsburg Monarchy participated).[214] Besides deriving from presumed superiority of the Italian and French idioms – musical and literary, respectively – the prejudice stemmed from the same origin as the disdain for lower social classes and religious dissenters: viewed as mere entertainment for the alien burghers, the German theatre seemed unworthy of attention. A meaningful example illustrating this deprecatory attitude comes from a note about the arrival of Constantini's actor-singers in a handwritten newspaper:

> Polish actors, having been disbanded in consequence of their entrepreneur's bankruptcy, moved to Lviv, and Germans imported from foreign countries began to perform, but nobody approves of them, so the theatre, built and until now maintained at considerable cost, is slackening off. The seigneurs ['Państwo'], not having for themselves decent entertainments, and especially in order to enjoy fresh air in the month of May, are leaving Warsaw en masse.[215]

The beginning of the first German season (1774–75) featuring Kurz in his by-then legendary comic role must have left the audience with mixed impressions. It is unlikely that Warsaw witnessed refined versions of the *Bernardoniaden* seasoned with *Arlekinade*, *Zauber*, and *Gaukelkunst* – recent Viennese revisions did little to prevent spontaneous farcical antics – although the interspersed arias (for instance, by Joseph Haydn in *Asmodeus, der krumme Teufel*) added to their artistic value.[216] Alluding to the title of *Das große Loos* (Bertuch – Wolf), the second and last North German Singspiel given at the end of the 1775–76 season (now under Ryx's management), Mitzler shared in the sentiment of the released German actor-singers' 'regretting that they drew the shortest lottery ticket [*Los*] in Warsaw'; the

---

[212] [Mitzler], *Vierter Brief*, 63; Philipp Johann Müller to Antoni Sułkowski, 15 October 1775 and Joseph Franz Alexi to Antoni Sułkowski, ca. 15 October 1775, Warsaw, ISPAN, AMR, 1067 59 (1), see in Rulikowski, *Warszawski teatr*, pp. 154–5, 202–3.

[213] [Mitzler], *Fünfter und letzter Brief*, 75.

[214] Salmonowicz, *Polacy i Niemcy wobec siebie*, pp. 21–30, 49–54.

[215] A handwritten newspaper from Warsaw, 7 May 1781, Warsaw, AGAD, AZ, 3063.

[216] Zechmeister, *Die Wiener Theater*, p. 53.

underappreciated merit of the troupe resided in introducing such valuable treasures of German literature as the bourgeois drama *Emilia Galotti* by Gotthold Ephraim Lessing.[217]

The bourgeois character of the German theatre in Warsaw explains why, despite the relatively high number of performances (for instance, three to four a week in 1781), we know only little about its musical offerings.[218] While it may seem surprising that no single report on the premiere of *Die Entführung aus dem Serail* – Warsaw's first Mozart opera – on 8 May 1783 has been found, this is due to absence of first-hand accounts from noble spectators, combined with only sporadic occurrences of professional theatrical criticism.

The performance on the king's name day indicates that it was a groundbreaking event all the same. Selection of repertoire for ceremonial festivities comprising a spectacle at the public venue, typically taking place between a sumptuous dinner and a ball, required royal approval and evoked general interest. This guaranteed both high income and prestige, all the more so because in the past Italian opera often took on a representative function, and was in any case considered most suited for anniversaries of the king's birthday (17 January), name day (8 May), election (7 September), and coronation (25 November): *Il viaggiatore ridicolo* (Goldoni – Gassman, 8 May 1775), *L'impresa d'opera* (Cavalieri – Guglielmi, 25 November 1775), and *L'amante di tutte* (A. Galuppi – B. Galuppi, 17 January 1776), among others. The character of the gala night, coinciding with the inauguration of a new season under the management of Lubomirski, was certainly glamorous. As various playbills confirm, the atmosphere at special performances was elevated through the ceremonial sound of trumpets and timpani. The theatre got fully illuminated with additional candles on two pendant chandeliers and the side brackets, which greatly pleased the audience. In all likelihood, spectators filled the venue to capacity, as was typically the case with royal celebrations, and received the Viennese novelty favourably, considering that it inspired Bogusławski to present a Polish adaptation only six months later. The performers – members of the former company assembled by Constantini, who went the extra mile in seeking the best possible singers – had sufficient skills to fit the bill, as suggested by their considerable experience and details of surviving contracts.[219]

In view of the unprecedentedly glamorous circumstances surrounding a German Singspiel, Warsaw's *Entführung* contributed to the stupendous effect of Mozart

---

[217] 'Die deutschen Komödianten sind zu bedauern, daß sie das kleinste Loos in Polen gezogen'. [Mitzler], *Fünfter und letzter Brief*, 88; [Mitzler], *Dritter Brief*, 47.

[218] Literally nothing is known about the second enterprise of Constantini that ended in spring 1785.

[219] For instance, Madame Hanke was obliged to take turns in performing leading roles with a *prima donna* in a planned Italian company, which shows she displayed a sufficient technique to impress in the favourite type of opera. Contract between Jerzy Marcin Lubomirski and the Hankes, 7 April 1783, Warsaw, ISPAN, AMR, 1067 63 (1).

opera despite only a single performance (followed by untimely collapse of Lubomirski's enterprise) and the nobility's previous aloofness. Similarly to *Die Zauberflöte* premiered by Bulla on 27 July 1793, however, it arrived by means of usual circulations of German-language works and performers within the established cultural and theatrical space, rather than on the wave of the composer's international fame. The initial dissemination of the two celebrated Viennese Singspiels illuminates Warsaw's significance not only within that space but also among the non-German (politically and administratively) participating cities. The *Entführung* had its second premiere in Strasbourg (January 1783) and, besides spreading to Warsaw and Prague around the same time (spring 1783), it was soon staged in Riga (February 1785). *Die Zauberflöte* which first travelled to Lviv (September 1792) and was taken by the same *Prinzipal* to Warsaw less than a year later, reached Gdańsk, Amsterdam (1794), Cracow (1796), Reval, Riga, and Saint Petersburg (1797) by the end of the century. A participator in the domain of German opera situated away from London and Paris, moreover, Stanislavian Warsaw provided a platform for non-canonical Singspiels that nevertheless played an enormous role in shaping German-language operatic traditions, among them the famous *Die Jagd* (Weisse – Hiller) given by Constantini and *Der Doktor und der Apotheker* (Stephanie – Dittersdorf), one of Vienna's favourite, put on by Bulla.

The first Warsaw production of *Die Zauberflöte* paralleled that in Lviv, but this relation could well be further extended. The extraordinary mobility within late eighteenth-century German theatre catalyzed multiple professional interconnections. Not all casts in the early performances of Mozart's Singspiels can be tracked down, but some of them indubitably featured Warsaw's former performers. Elise Fournier, for example, sang again in *Die Zauberflöte* in the season of 1796–97 while in Cracow as an actress-singer in a troupe of Karl Wothe, previously also Bulla's performer in Warsaw.[220] The return of the tenor Arnold to Vienna in 1785 coincided with the National Singspiel's revival of the *Entführung*, in which he was Warsaw's Belmonte. The experience attained at the Polish capital was valuable, even to a number of highly qualified Italian singers whose professional paths criss-crossed the continent. Guardasoni took the operas that he first produced on the Warsaw public stage in the 1790–91 season (e.g., *Zenobia di Palmira*, Sertor – Anfossi and *Pirro*, De Gamerra – Paisiello) to Prague and Leipzig, while the core members of his troupe – Baglioni and Campi, the future first performers in Mozart's *La clemenza di Tito* – left Warsaw with newly acquired skills necessary for singing in *opera seria* thanks to the entrepreneur's unprecedented involvement in the serious genre.[221] Warsaw's presence on

---

[220] Got, *Das österreichische Theater in Krakau*, p. 26.
[221] Rice, *Mozart on the Stage*, pp. 126–8, 133–4; Rice, 'Antonio Baglioni', p. 28.

the operatic map of Europe had remarkable consequences; rather than one-sidedly beneficial, it was universally worthwhile.

5 Opera and Urban Life

5.1 A City of Urban Transition

'Here in Warsaw, one always wants what is new, and even when it sometimes also happens to be bad, in the first place it is good just because it is new', observed Mitzler.[222] Opera's presence alone did not suffice to please; the notion of novelty in particular inspired efforts to make operatic offerings as attractive as possible. Exempted from direct royal patronage after the First Partition, the Warsaw public theatre entered a phase characterized by entrepreneurs' increased efforts to lure and entrance spectators – a spectrum of Warsaw's inhabitants and visitors rather than a narrow elite circle.

The audience obtained an active voice in choosing the repertoire and judging the singers. Within a relatively short distance separating the spectators from the performers, who remained mostly right behind the footlights, reactions in the auditorium determined future performances on a daily basis. A hierarchy of operatic genres emerged spontaneously, thereby exerting an impact on entrepreneurial undertakings. '[T]he *publicum* demands and claims Italian opera spectacles as often as possible,' wrote Ryx in business-related correspondence in 1774.[223] Rare appearances of *opera seria* caught attention amid festive surroundings. *Opéra-comique* pleased the high nobility identifying with the social francophone dimension, but eventually fell prey to the disposition of the majority unenchanted by the French singing. German opera languished in the lowest rank of musical spectacles, although it outlived the French performances.

As permanent home to Polish actor-singers and a host to the foreign companies, the public stage continued to fulfil its Enlightenment mission, although vagaries of theatrical and operatic businesses affected operagoing, and vice versa. Unpredictable situations: financial failure (Bessesti, Lubomirski in 1785), cancellation of a lease of a theatre building (Montbrun), and even mysterious intrigues (Lubomirski in 1783) forced the entrepreneurs (and their financial partners) to quit prematurely. The policy telling the troupes to perform on preordained days of week would have been less problematic if every day in the theatrical calendar was equally 'valuable', but in fact Sunday evenings

---

[222] 'Man will hier in Warschau immer was neues haben, und wann es manchmal auch schlecht ist, so ist es doch zum ersten mal gut, weil es was neues ist'. [Mitzler], *Brief*, 3.

[223] 'Publicum żąda i dopomina się jak najczęściej opery włoskiej', François Ryx to Antoni Tyzenhauz, 4 January 1775, Warsaw, AGAD, AT, F 23. See in Wierzbicka-Michalska, 'Scena', pp. 784–5.

remained the most popular time for visiting the theatre. In summer, when landowners relocated to their countryside estates, Warsaw's theatrical activity slowed significantly. The singers' departures started to coincide with the nobility's exodus (the former employees of Bessesti and Gaillard); another tactic was to delay the season openings until September (Hamon, Lubomirski, Ryx, and Guardasoni). Moreover, the realities in the city deprived of a strong burgher stratum were such that box subscribers – regular theatregoers – dictated frequent premieres and fewer repetitions. The hire of competent singers, particularly enthralling *prime donne* demanded by the audience, strained budgets but nevertheless constituted the foremost prerequisite of success. In light of the Warsaw audience's fondness for ballets, a fortune spent on adorning performance nights with eye-catching dances paid off.

The king provided support, either directly or through exchange of services securing the finances of the monopoly holder Ryx. Wishing to interfere with vital decisions, he wanted his trusted man to stay on the job. A contract of Lubomirski, for example, envisioned free exploitation of the public theatre and its inventory, as well as coverage of the singers' dwellings, in return of concerts for the court. The king's extensive subscription to boxes was paid back by Guardasoni and Pellatti's singers performing at the royal residencies, including the king's suburban Łazienki Palace equipped with a small court theatre and a large amphitheatre.[224]

The expanded participation of the theatre performers in Warsaw's life was nothing new, all the same. The French actor-singers performed jointly with nobles at sumptuous *théâtres de société*, for example that of King Poniatowski's antagonist Primate Gabriel Podoski where cosmopolitan theatrical life concentrated for several months after the departure of Rousselois (1769).[225] The vocal talents of Tomatis's Italian singers got a broader exposure at outdoor festivities.[226] The disparate worlds of actors and high society frequently converged while also exceeding noble patronage; an important common ground was membership in Freemasonic lodges, among which one founded in 1766 by Moszyński and other people close to the king convened for the first time at Rousselois's apartment.[227] The German actor-singers in Constantini's troupe sang at public concerts as well as in church, and even committed to charity performances in support of fire victims at Warsaw's suburb Praga.[228] Lastly, the

---

[224] Wierzbicka-Michalska, *Sześć studiów o teatrze*, pp. 67–99.

[225] Klimowicz, *Początki teatru*, pp. 370–5.

[226] Jackl, 'Teatr stanisławowski', 54; Klimowicz, *Początki teatru*, pp. 126–9.

[227] Hass, *Sekta farmazonii warszawskiej*, pp. 69, 109–11.

[228] 'Journal du théâtre de Varsovie commencée de l'année 1781', Cracow, BJ, 6118 II, see in Bernacki, *Teatr, dramat i muzyka*, vol. 1, p. 218; *Annonces et Avis Divers de Varsovie*, no. 9 (24 August 1782), 3–4; Jackl, 'Teatr i życie teatralne', p. 535.

Italian and French singers appearing on the public stage provided singing lessons, very desired among high-born ladies attending opera, across the city.[229]

These recurring manifestations of invigorated cultural life, stemming from the continuous character of the public theatre, were factors in the rise of Warsaw as Poland's important urban centre. By contrast, the elaborate theatrical events organized during the Saxon decades (1699–1763) elevated the cultural significance of the Polish capital only during the sporadic arrivals of the former two rulers, for whom the court of Dresden remained the preferable residence. In view of the centuries-long crisis of underdeveloped and weakly populated Polish towns, combined with the predominance of countryside noble culture, Warsaw's speedy metamorphosis was revolutionary. Indeed, the momentous establishment of the institutionalized theatrical activities that induced consumption of cultural goods by people from different strata helped to move social and cultural life back to urban space.[230]

The city's energy pulsated through the crowded theatrical surroundings. The Saxon Garden next to *Operalnia* became a place of pleasant social gatherings before and after the spectacles beginning at 6 pm.[231] Special performances sometimes moved outdoors for fireworks and other attractions.[232] The theatre building raised by Ryx (1779) stood in the heart of Warsaw's newly emerging intellectual-administrative centre around the Krasiński Square, opposite the stately Krasiński Palace with its busy public garden, and in the vicinity of the utilitarian and educational institutions such as the Załuski Library and the Piarist-run Collegium Nobilium.[233] Commonly referred to as *Teatr Narodowy* ('National Theatre'), the cramped (and gradually extended rather chaotically) building designed by Bonaventura Solari served its purpose until 1833, when a sharper division between 'low' and 'high' genres required a separate venue for cultivation of opera.[234]

As there was no large market for specialized periodicals in Poland, only three theatrical journals, all short-lived experiments, commented on Warsaw's theatrical and operatic life: Mitzler's *Briefe* (1775–76), *Kalendarz Teatrowy* (*The Theatre Calendar*, 1779), and *Theatralisches Quodlibet für Schauspieler und Schauspiielliebhaber* (1782–83) by Gottlieb Lorenz (an actor in Constantini's troupe). Nevertheless, the rise of programmatic and journalistic writings concerning theatre (e.g., in the *Monitor*), followed by pioneering reviews of the Warsaw

---

[229] Magier, *Estetyka miasta*, pp. 110–11.   [230] See Zajas, 'The Ambiguous Republic', p. 19.

[231] This gave a lot of opportunity for the Saxon spy Heine to overhear interesting conversations; Klimowicz, 'Repertuar teatru', 238.

[232] Jackl, 'Teatr stanisławowski', 33, 71.   [233] Janowski, *Narodziny inteligencji*, p. 43.

[234] The name was not officially bestowed on the theatre. Warsaw playbills did not include the heading 'Teatr Narodowy' until as late as 1814, and even then (1814–33) the phrase stood for the Polish theatrical company rather than the venue itself, see Raszewski, *Trudny rebus*, pp. 57–60.

productions in the *Journal Littéraire de Varsovie,* was groundbreaking: it fore-shadowed professional theatrical criticism. Although the most circulated news-paper *Gazeta Warszawska* (*The Warsaw Gazette,* 1774–93) did not serve for a regular written contact between the public stage and the theatregoers, day-to-day communication existed through on-stage announcements and informative playbills (bilingual for foreign-language events). Bogusławski, in particular, championed direct confrontation with the spectators after the performances, during which his future undertakings clarified in accord with the reactions; all entrepreneurs used playbills to praise the performers and apologize for shortcom-ings. Opera and urban life coexisted and overlapped, thereby exerting reciprocal effects.

5.2 Novelties, Novelties

From a commercial point of view, the periodic character of the enterprises had an important advantage: it contributed to an aura of excitement each time new Italian singers arrived in town. The inauguration of the 1784–85 season caused a flutter – three entire years had elapsed since the sojourn of the previous Italian troupe. Overjoyed at the reappearance of *opera buffa*, the nobility proclaimed the members of the Zappa company 'the most sonorous and excellent voices ever heard in Warsaw', although they were in fact no more accomplished than their predecessors.[235]

Otherwise, the entrepreneurs of *opera buffa* felt much pressure to keep the public involved with novelties or, at least, by alternating operas. This emanates from Guardasoni's apology for repeating *Il pittore parigino* (Petrosellini – Cimarosa) – two days after a previous performance and for the fifth time within two weeks – instead of introducing a new work.[236] The hectic dynamics of the 1789–90 and 1790–91 Italian seasons encompassing at least twenty-five inter-mingling titles, including nineteen premieres, contrasted with the initial practice of exploiting a single *opera buffa* for about a month, until another one was ready for staging. The newly premiered operas satisfied curiosity, but their stage longevity entirely depended on favourable reception; Mitzler's definition of a flop was a new Italian opera without at least four repetitions.[237] The spectators greatly enjoyed sentimental *opere buffe* while also expected a variety. A potpourri

---

[235] A handwritten newspaper from Vilnius, 14 April 1784, in Jackl, 'Teatr i życie teatralne', pp. 552–3. Gaillard joined (or replaced) Zappa later in the season; details of this entrepreneurial partnership remain unknown.

[236] Playbill announcement of *Il pittore parigino*, 13 September 1790, in Bernacki, *Teatr, dramat i muzyka*, vol 1, p. 336; Playbill for *Il pittore parigino*, 15 September 1790, Warsaw, BN, SD XVIII.4.864.

[237] [Mitzler], *Vierter Brief,* 61.

presented for the closure of Pellatti's enterprise – something of a tradition by then – gave the last taste of the season's favourite: the comic *L'impresario in angustie* (Diodati – Cimarosa), the pastoral *La virtuosa bizzarra* (Zini – Guglielmi), and the sentimental *La cifra* (Da Ponte – Salieri).[238]

Vocal display often worked to the benefit of repetitions, nevertheless, because a novelty not only meant an opera newly arrived in Warsaw, but also embraced enthralling extras: additional arias, guest appearances, and various embellishments incorporated into well-known settings. As a number of playbills suggest, surprising elements intrigued regular theatregoers. One novel way of pleasing the audience that came to the forefront during Guardasoni's enterprise was an emphasis on 'large choruses', routinely advertised as particularly attractive elements of the spectacles.[239] Indeed, expressive choral sounds fulfilled a substantial dramatic function in *Axur*, everyone's favourite *tragicomico* opera.

The modifications might be inspired by a local taste shaped by domestic musical traditions. As noted by perceptive Schulz,

> The liking for music in Warsaw is common, especially among the high born … although [even] the noblest ones do not have enough knowledge of it and true appreciation. What one sings in the company, and dances to, falls within the spirit of the nation.[240]

The Italian singers learned to adjust to the preference of familiar sounds, and occasionally gave their operas a dab of Polish colour. Simple tricks such as inclusion of stylized polonaises caused profound effects. An aria *alla polacca* performed by the first tenor Guardasoni was likely the most memorable fragment of *La sposa fedele*.[241] An additional 'Polish' aria of unknown provenance that Rosa Bernardi, a soprano hired during Sułkowski's enterprise, sang in the audience's beloved *Il finto pazzo per amore* (Mariani – Sacchini) reached pinnacles of popularity far and wide.[242] The tenor Lazzerini (the Zappa-Gaillard troupe) went a step further by adorning the second act of *Le gelosie villane* (Grandi – Sarti) with 'a Polish aria of his own composition', whereas the tenor Antonio Palmini even challenged himself to perform an aria in Polish on the last night of the Pellatti company. A newly employed soprano in the troupe of Guardasoni, Anna Paccini, strived to earn favour performing an additional

---

[238] Playbill announcement, 31 May 1793, in Bernacki, *Teatr, dramat i muzyka*, vol. 1, p. 377.

[239] Texts of Warsaw playbills, Warsaw, ISPAN, AMR, 1067 60 (2).

[240] 'Der Geschmack an der Musik ist in Warschau allgemein, vorzüglich aber in den höhern Ständen … So sehr man indessen die Musik liebt, fehlt es doch an einer Kenntniß der edleren und erhabenern, und an wahrem Gefallen daran. Diejenige, die man in Gesellschaft singt, und nach der man tanzen kann, sagt dem Geiste der Nation mehr zu'. [Schulz], *Reise eines Liefländers*, vol. 4, pp. 61–2.

[241] [Mitzler], *Brief*, 13.   [242] Bogusławski, *Dzieje Teatru Narodowego*, p. 8.

'Polish' number in *Fra i due litiganti il terzo gode*. On her benefit night, Pellatti's *prima donna* Anna Benini supplemented *La virtuosa bizzarra* with 'a little Polish aria of gratefulness for indulgence and favours [she met with] in this capital city'.[243] The endeavours to flatter the Warsaw audience complied with specificity of a moment.

The rediscovery of *opera seria*, 'the unknown type of singing' (as Bogusławski put it) since the last Saxon spectacle (1763), created a sensation in 1776. One reason was the rarity of castratos in Warsaw. *Didone abbandonata* (Metastasio – Anfossi) featuring Bonafini and Compagnucci, so contrasting with the by now – at the end of the second season after the theatre's reopening – overfamiliar *opera buffa*, gave a fresh sparkle to the public theatre:

> The serious opera pleased enormously and completely overshadowed the *opera buffa*. So many spectators came to the first performance [on 29 February 1776] that some, not having found a seat, had to go back. The music by Mr. Anfossi is good; the stage decorations are also well suited.[244]

This and the successive offerings: *Demofoonte* (Metastasio – Anfossi) and *Orfeo ed Euridice* deeply engraved in Bogusławski's memory:

> It is hard to describe, and even more difficult to believe – except for those who remember – how ecstatically this unknown type of singing was received. The ubiquitous enthusiasm of the public could only be compared with the nearly superhuman adoration that propelled Greece into erecting monuments to immortal glory of Olympic wrestlers. Tripled prices for all seats did not hold back the curious crowd.[245]

It was not chance that the attention-catching shift towards the serious genre coincided with the king's return to the public eye following the First Partition and Ryx's takeover of the theatre management from Kurz. Royal financial contributions – including direct, generous patronage over Bonafini and Compagnucci – enabled an expensive venture normally rather incompatible with the nature of the impresarial theatre. Thus, the operatic premieres adorned important royal anniversaries, whereas the king capitalized on having both

---

[243] See playbill announcements in Bernacki, *Teatr, dramat i muzyka*, vol. 1, pp. 273, 325, 328, 376–7.

[244] 'Diese ernsthafte Oper hat ungemein gefallen, und die Opera Buffa völlig verdunkelt. Es sind so so viele Zuschauer zum erstenmal gewesen, daß einige wieder zurück gekehrt, weil sie keinen Platz gefunden. Die Musik ist gut, von Hrn. Anfossi, die Verzierungen des Theaters gleichfalls wohl angebracht'. [Mitzler], *Fünfter und letzter Brief*, 86.

[245] 'Trudno jest opisać, trudniey jeszcze uwierzyć, chyba tym którzy to pamiętają z jakiem uniesieniem przyjętym został ten nieznaiomy dotąd rodzaj śpiewania. Powszechny naówczas zapał Publiczności, nieledwoby porównać można z owem nadludzkiem prawie uwielbieniem, z iakiem niegdyś Grecya dla zapaśników Olimpiiskich widowisk stawiała posągi ku nieśmiertelney ich sławie! W troynasób pomnożona opłata weyścia na wszystkie mieysca, nie wstrzymywała ciekawych'. Bogusławski, *Dzieje Teatru Narodowego*, pp. 11–12.

admirable operas and singers to bolster a publicity strategy. The serious operas did more than magnify his royal majesty: they helped to build authority by the non-hereditary, replaceable monarch determined to thrust forward unpopular reforms. By virtue of engaging Bonafini, who had been Anfossi's original Didone in the 1775 premiere at Teatro San Moisè, King Poniatowski's ambition went as far as replicating the effect of a recent Venetian production. In return for sponsoring Marchesi, the talk of the town for nearly two weeks in March 1785 whose voice, heard at private royal concerts and the public theatre, took the audiences by storm, the king won attention of the cosmopolitan nobility. As announced on a playbill, 'Mr. Marchesini, just as in other countries [where he had won] considerable respect and favours, received significant commendation in this capital'.[246] Ryx's enterprise in the 1786–87 season, the only one entirely dedicated to *opera seria*, again pivoted around virtuosos in royal service: Brigida Banti – then at the peak of her international career – and castrato Pietro Benedetti (Sartorino).[247] The other entrepreneurs faced the demand for *opera seria* by overcoming vocal limitations of the available *buffi*; Guardasoni and Pellatti even did without castratos by transposing male vocal parts to lower registers, and perhaps modifying them melodically.[248] Premiered on royal festive days, these *opere serie* mostly coincided with the period of the sociopolitical upliftment during the parliamentary works on the Constitution of 3 May 1791. The king did not miss the opportunity to celebrate his role as the enlightened proponent of the reformist laws with a finale chorus scene in *Zenobia di Palmira* (Sertor – Anfossi) where a scenery of shining clouds opened slowly to reveal the name 'Stanislao Augusto' in luminous capital letters.[249] The dominant ambience in the auditorium must have been similar to the enthusiasm accompanying the better documented premiere of the political play *Powrót posła* (*The Return of the Deputy*) by Niemcewicz only two days earlier. Surrounded with festivity, the serious productions produced an atmosphere of carnivalesque rejoicing; Marchesi's last appearance in *Giulio Sabino* concluded with a grand masked ball at the public theatre, 'honouring the famous virtuoso' as if he was a crowned head.[250] This was in tune with *opera seria*'s inherent associations

---

[246] 'Pan Marchesini, jak w innych krajach niemały szacunek i względy, tak przy pierwszej reprezentacyi ... podobnież w tutejszej stolicy przyzwoitą swego osobliwego talentu pozyskał pochwałę'. Playbill announcement of *Giulio Sabino*, 19 March 1785, in Bernacki, *Teatr, dramat i muzyka*, vol. 1, p. 279.

[247] Playbill for *Ariarate*, 11 January 1787, Warsaw, MT.

[248] Ryszka-Komarnicka, 'From Venice to Warsaw', pp. 301–5.

[249] *Zenobia di Palmira* (Warsaw: Dufour, 1791).

[250] Playbill announcement of *Giulio Sabino*, 25 September 1785, in Bernacki, *Teatr, dramat i muzyka*, vol. 1, p. 280.

with jolly celebration.[251] Except that such elevated events in operatic life of Warsaw were independent of a fixed calendar. If *opera buffa* was a feast, the scattered occurrences of *opera seria* resembled extended Carnivals.

But not even the most ardent fascinations ruled unconditionally, and disappointment called for immediate revisions. A second performance of *Elpinice* (? – Giordani) in which Banti's talent shone brightly was advertised as properly corrected, and likewise a repetition of *Alessandro nell'Indie* (Metastasio – Bianchi), premiered by Pellatti amid the turbulence of the Targowica Confederation (1792) that preceded the Second Partition, had to be shortened and given new arias 'in accordance with the wishes of the audience'.[252] The voice of the *publicum* prevailed for every operatic genre.

5.3 The Price of Stardom

'Yesterday, Banti gave us *Elpinice*, a rather bad and meaningless opera, but containing several beautiful arias', wrote the king's niece Urszula Mniszchowa in a private letter about the production ending the *seria* season.[253] The Italian singers, the *seria* stars in particular, stood at the centre of the operatic events, superior to the operas' creators, and even the operas themselves. Entrancing singing did have the power to overcome flaws in plots, musical composition, and orchestral playing. No wonder the frontal singers aroused interest among the nobility. In the same letter, Mniszchowa informs the addressee of Banti's planned departure for Vienna in a style normally reserved for gossiping about members of highest noble circles. A handwritten newspaper abounds in news about mysterious intrigues surrounding the return of Bonafini from Saint Petersburg (1782); the anonymous author reckoned, for example, the readers would like to know that Compagnucci 'died of sorrow after she left him'.[254] News concerning singers' exorbitant remunerations thrilled the nobles in particular. Soon before his arrival in Warsaw, Marchesi was rumoured to have made a fortune singing in Vienna; neither did an astronomical salary promised to him in Saint Petersburg escape notice.[255] Even if prone to exaggeration, the sources were well informed. Bonafini, repeatedly reported to be surrounded with luxury of her Warsaw residence, a stagecoach, several servants, and even

---

[251] See Rice, *Mozart on the Stage*, pp. 22–31.

[252] Playbill announcements of *Alessandro nell'Indie*, 10 October 1792 and *Elpinice*, 30 January 1787, in Bernacki, *Teatr, dramat i muzyka*, vol. 1, pp. 295, 357.

[253] Urszula Mniszchowa to Ludwika Zomoyska, 22 January 1787, in Zawadzki, 'Teatr we wspomnieniach', p. 654.

[254] A handwritten newspaper from Warsaw, 4 July 1782, Cracow, BCz, 2037, see in Jackl, 'Teatr i życie teatralne', p. 534.

[255] A handwritten newspaper from Warsaw, 7 September 1785 and 21 September 1785, Kórnik, BK, 1328, see in Jackl, 'Teatr i życie teatralne', p. 566.

a private harpsichordist replacing the royal composer Albertini at the weekly private concerts, was indeed rewarded generously. Not only was the soprano leading a glamorous life in Warsaw and enjoyed special favours under the king's patronage, but also displayed celebrity-like behaviour. Her first concert at the Royal Castle turned into a scandal after she refused to sing in front of persons from outside the royal family. Bonafini

> made so many frowns that she offended both his Majesty and the present ladies.... . Having taken her scores, she is ready to leave. The chamberlain follows her and asks to return, but she tosses herself around and complains about a broken agreement. In the end, the ladies themselves entreat her [to sing], then the king comes up and shows so much attention that all the ladies get hurt.[256]

The incident reminiscent of an *opera buffa* scene would have been unthinkable at the public theatre. Celebrity, this unconditional appraisal of famous singers, was not yet at its peak. Amidst all the dazzling excitement, the noble audience members held a far more privileged position in the relationship between them and the singers. What happened to the internationally praised soprano Banti at the beginning of her Warsaw season demonstrates strikingly a power asymmetry rather contradictory to our preconceptions about operatic divas. The prevalence of noble operagoers and the rules governing commercial theatre tempered the *prima donna*'s caprices. As publicized by *Gazeta Warszawska*, Banti took the liberty to interrupt a performance of *Ariarate* (Moretti – Tarchi) in order to express discontent at seeing someone in a second-floor box scoffing at her vocal efforts. Worse, having been immediately booed, she left the stage ostentatiously. No less a figure than Great Lithuanian Marshal Władysław Gurowski intervened on behalf of the offended nobles by ordering the singer to return and thoroughly apologize. She did so, and an escalation of the conflict was prevented. The next day, a resolution prohibiting the performers from upsetting the spectators, to whom they 'owed respect as those guaranteeing an income', came into being.[257] In fact, this was a manifest against violation of the noble pride. Back in July 1775, the first *buffo* Guardasoni found himself at the centre of a social scandal that put the Italian spectacles on hold for entire five days after some nobles in the parterre had reasons to take offense at his modified aria text in *L'isola di Alcina* (Bertati – Gazzaniga). At first stubborn, the singer eventually apologized publicly, while the management issued a special note forbidding unauthorized changes to the allocated parts.[258]

---

[256] A handwritten newspaper from Warsaw, 18 July 1782, and 1 August 1782, Cracow, BCz, 2037, see in Jackl, 'Teatr i życie teatralne', pp. 535–6.

[257] *Gazeta Warszawska*, no. 74 (16 September 1786), 1–2.

[258] [Mitzler], *Dritter Brief*, 46; Warsaw, ISPAN, AMR, 1067 59 (1), see in Rulikowski, *Warszawski teatr*, pp. 107–8, 112.

In confrontational situations with the audience, provoked or accidental, the singers had no choice but to accept their social inferiority.

The star stature had other privileges. Unlike the *buffi* dependant on the entrepreneurs' decisions and adaptable to fast working mode, the celebrated *seria* performers were so closely identified with their signature operatic roles that they often reappeared in the same repertoire across Europe. King Poniatowski wished to hear – and let the Warsaw audience hear – the invited *cantanti* perform their famous operatic parts in the first place.[259] Quite emotionally, but also perceptively, the operagoers indulged in the sensible peculiarity of Marchesi's singing in *Giulio Sabino* – the famous 'Marchesi effect' taking hold over the audiences in Milan, Vienna, and other opera centres, on the wave of sentimentalism.[260] The most acclaimed castrato of his time entranced Warsaw by the perfection of his vocal skills combined with exceptionally good acting. In contrast to other *seria* singers striving to please merely with techniques of their voices, Marchesi also 'had the talent to bring tears to the eyes of the spectators'.[261]

The Warsaw audience anticipated singing enriched with enthralling qualities; evidence reaching the beginnings of the public stage shows that good acting was one such characteristic. Domenico Poggi (performing with the Tomatis company in the 1766–67 season) and the star Bonafini received applause for presenting their operatic roles convincingly. A reason why the *basso buffo caricato* Giambattista Brocchi (a member of the Bessesti, Zappa-Gaillard and Lubomirski companies) earned everyone's admiration was his comic flair.[262] The tenor Baglioni (from Guardasoni's troupe) attracted attention by combining masterful singing with equally impressive acting.[263] It was in accord with both contemporaneous critique and the eclectic nature of the Warsaw public theatre that professional acting constituted an intrinsic element of the ideal opera performance. The singers who in many ways proved themselves worthy of admiration were even idolized. Literary men wrote sonnets applauding their talents and portraying the *prime donne* as quasi-goddesses possessing supernatural vocal capabilities; the author of the first Polish Enlightenment comedy Józef Bielawski dedicated one to Bonafini, more followed for Marchesi, Banti, and Baglioni. As recounted by Schulz, nearly every performance of Anna Benini, the *prima donna* in Pellatti's company, ended with a cascade of poems, in both Polish and Italian, falling to the parterre.[264]

---

[259] Parkitna, 'Pursuing Enlightenment Delights', pp. 59–60.

[260] Rice, 'Sense, Sensibility, and Opera Seria', 101–38.

[261] Bogusławski, *Dzieje Teatru Narodowego*, p. 51; Bogusławski, 'Uwagi nad operą *Jozef w Egiptcie*', p. 358.

[262] Bogusławski, *Dzieje Teatru Narodowego*, p. 32.   [263] *Theater-Kalender* 19 (1793), 146.

[264] [Schulz], *Reise eines Liefländers*, vol. 4, p. 75.

The female singers were all the more vulnerable to public judgement due to long-time associations of their theatrical profession with sexual availability. As late as 1792, Schulz classified Warsaw's actresses and dancers, whose lifestyles paralleled those of their peers in Paris, Venice, Naples, or Livorno, into the category of canny prostitutes.[265] Although biased, the claim wraps off an unspoken reality. The king's sexual relationship with Bonafini was well known to everybody, yet went unmentioned in gossiping about the jealous torment of the royal mistress Elżbieta Grabowska.[266] Instead of prudishness, this was courteous discretion. On the contrary, meticulous comments about the outer features of the women on stage were commonplace. Needless to say, rivalry supplied fuel for constant comparisons. The two renowned sopranos, Benini and Adriana Ferrarese del Bene, who competed for primacy in Pellatti's troupe, received applause from different supporting camps on the basis of vocal preferences as well as superficial judgements of their looks.[267]

The special ambience surrounding Italian spectacles translated into amateur performances of *opera buffa*. We know of at least three private stagings of Paisiello's works by Warsaw's *nobili dilettanti*: *La modista raggiratrice* (initiated by Michał Kazimierz Ogiński in September 1789), as well as *Nina, o sia La pazza per amore* and *La serva padrona*.[268] While all coincided with the enterprise of Guardasoni, the last two must have been directly inspired by the Italian company's current repertoire. However, the francophone nobility took particular pleasure in amateur *théâtres de société* featuring French-language works, including *opéra-comique* whose affiliation with French spoken theatre opened the door to support by the exclusive circles – as it turned out, too exclusive in light of the changing realities of the Warsaw public stage.

5.4 The Audience Decides

'Only the [Russian] Ambassador, his clique, and Duchess Lubomirska, as well as some other ladies, enjoy the French spectacles; most of the spectators prefer the national theatre, the ballets, and Italian opera,' observed Moszyński towards the end of Hamon's second season.[269] Ostensibly, the *opéras-comiques* attracted more theatregoers than the spoken plays because the latter – particularly tragedies – could only be understood by those knowing the French language very

---

[265] [Schulz], *Reise eines Liefländers*, vol. 3, p. 70.

[266] A handwritten newspaper from Warsaw, 15 August 1782 and 12 September 1782, Cracow, BCz, 2037, see in Jackl, 'Teatr i życie teatralne', p. 537

[267] [Schulz], *Reise eines Liefländers*, vol. 4, pp. 74–6.

[268] Bernacki, *Teatr, dramat i muzyka*, vol. 1, pp. 272–3; [Czacki], *Wspomnienie z roku*, p. 115.

[269] August Moszyński to August (?) Sułkowski, 19 January 1778, Warsaw, ISPAN, AMR, 1067 59 (1), see in Rulikowski, *Warszawski teatr*, pp. 214–7.

well.[270] Noisy incidents in the auditorium escalated;[271] the delicate singing voice of Mademoiselle Dufrenoy fared badly against the cacophony of the parterre.[272] A tremendous rumbling during a performance of Denis Diderot's play *Le père de famille* faded only after the king showed up during the fourth act.[273]

Warsaw's high nobility made a particularly receptive audience of the resident French companies. A special relation between these theatregoers, eagerly contributing money towards installing French theatrical projects, and French-language repertoire shaped Hamon's fortune. The entrepreneur won general approval for his troupe; Prince Michał Kazimierz Ogiński, the Grand Hetman of Lithuania and an agile composer, thought it 'quite good', whereas Jacek Ogrodzki, a royal official, described Hamon and Saint-Huberty's opening with *L'ami de la maison* and *Les deux avares* (Fenouillot de Falbaire – Grétry) as 'deserving applause'.[274] However, he once approached a disaster by offending the nobles with increased ticket prices and prompting some glamorous ladies to move to the parterre in a gesture of disapproval.[275] The rivalry between two talented sopranos, Madame Hamon and the younger Antoinette Saint-Huberty – the future Parisian star in Gluck opera – provided additional amusement. The prevalence of works by the early generation of *opéra-comique* composers: Duni, Monsigny, and Philidor during the 1777–78 season reflected entrepreneurial alertness to expectations; *Rose et Colas*, *Les deux chasseurs et la laitière*, and *La clochette* (Anseaume – Duni) were fashionable as they remained among Paris's most favourite titles throughout all of the 1770s.[276] Even though the critics writing for the *Journal Littéraire de Varsovie* championed more recent Parisian stage works and a greater repertoire variety, they also reported with satisfaction about a commendable level of Warsaw performances of *Le peintre amoureux de son modèle* and *Le maréchal ferrant*, previously introduced here as far back as twelve years ago.[277]

This prolonged success, clearly contrasting with the thrust for Italian novelties, demonstrates the extent to which Warsaw's French-speaking elite appropriated and celebrated some Parisian canonical works, thereby becoming one driving force behind dissemination of *opéra-comique*.[278] The revival of *Rose et Colas*, 'that little piece, which almost everybody knows by heart', was received with general applause.[279] The audience well acquainted with the repeatedly

---

[270] Wierzbicka-Michalska, *Aktorzy cudzoziemscy*, p. 78.   [271] Ibid., p. 96.

[272] See an excerpt from the *Journal Littéraire de Varsovie* in Bernacki, *Teatr, dramat i muzyka*, vol. 1, p. 142.

[273] Ibid., p. 140.

[274] Wierzbicka-Michalska, 'Scena', p. 802; Wierzbicka-Michalska, *Aktorzy cudzoziemscy*, p. 78.

[275] Jackl, 'Teatr stanisławowski', 35.   [276] See Charlton, *Grétry and the Growth*, p. 66.

[277] *Journal Littéraire de Varsovie* (3rd issue of June 1777), 229; *Journal Littéraire de Varsovie* (2nd issue of February 1778), 239–40.

[278] See Markovits, *Staging Civilization*, pp. 72–83.

[279] 'Cette petite pièce que presque tout le monde sait par cœur a été accueilli avec des applaudissements universels'. *Journal Littéraire de Varsovie* (3rd issue of January 1778), 142.

performed *Les deux chasseurs et la laitière*, 'whose music is excellent', always found it pleasant.[280] Equipped by rich experience, Hamon ultimately invested most efforts into sustaining interest of worldly nobles identifying themselves with the French repertoire that they were also gladly exploring at the *théâtres de société*; we know, for example, of an amateur production of *Rose et Colas* that predated Hamon's revival of this opera on the public stage.[281] It was no small segment of visitors to the public theatre whose predilections became the target; the number of tickets distributed for an amateur French performance at the Royal Castle in 1782, for example, reached 200.[282] In parallel, the *Journal Littéraire de Varsovie* claimed that

> the continued success of all our little *opéras-comiques* across Europe should oblige the directors of spectacles to satisfy this taste, if the public so decides, and to present often these light productions, which please infinitely due to their cheerful and picturesque character.[283]

In a long run, however, imparting a special importance to preferences of the audience spurred a process replacing the will of the privileged with a more democratic diversion. French spectacles, so firmly woven into the social life of the noble circles that considered something of their own, did not withstand the commands of the public theatre succumbing to the expectations of the general audience. For what looks on the pages of the francophone periodical like a manifestation of a universal taste was eventually outweighed by a taste of the majority.

Warsaw spectators did not, generally speaking, admire French singing in the same way they praised Italian virtuosity. The difference between the two was perceived through dissimilar vocal techniques and musical styles. As explained by Moszyński to troubled Villiers, whose unfit productions of *opéra-comique* caused utmost dissatisfaction in 1765, not only the lack of good French actor-singers represented a challenge, but also the fact that the Polish nation inclined towards Italian, rather than French, music to which it had grown accustomed throughout many years.[284] Ingrained musical preferences manifested through heightened sensitivity towards a 'peculiar' method of singing, typically described

---

[280] *Journal Littéraire de Varsovie* (3rd issue of February 1778), 272; *Journal Littéraire de Varsovie* (1st issue of January 1778), 63.

[281] Czartoryski, *Memoirs of Prince*, vol. 1, p. 26.

[282] A handwritten newspaper from Warsaw, 25 December 1782, quoted in Jackl, 'Teatr i życie teatralne', p. 538.

[283] '[L]e succès toujours soutenu qu'ont dans toute l'Europe nos petits opéras comiques devrait engager les directeurs de spectacles à satisfaire ce goût si décidé du public et à lui présenter souvent ces productions légères qui plaisent infiniment par la gaieté et par le pittoresque de leur caractère'. *Journal Littéraire de Varsovie* (3rd issue of January 1778), 142.

[284] 'Vous n'ignorez pas que la nation est plus tot portée pour la musique italiene, que pour la francoise, puis qu'elle y est accoutumée depuis tant d'années'. Moszyński to the troupe directed by Villiers, AGAD, AJP, 444, see in Wierzbicka, *Źródła do historii teatru*, vol. 1, p. 21.

as 'screaming' and 'bawling'. Kazimierz Ustrzycki, a young noble man, praised Hamon's production of *Henri IV, ou La bataille d'Ivry* (Durosoy – Martini) only because he ascribed superior properties to the music by (as he wrongly assumed) an Italian-born composer:

> The music of this opera, composed by an Italian, is superb; if only those French devils had wanted to bawl a little less, the entire spectacle would have been charming.[285]

The bias had a strong effect; the French musical style did not assimilate easily into Warsaw's theatrical life. Even music to a ballet (*Bacchus et Ariane*, 1791) by the composer Jean-Baptiste Rochefort was considered 'not best for the Warsaw ears' because it contained 'a lot of scream-like French features'; for that reason, it was entirely replaced with a setting by a local composer.[286] Bogusławski dismissed the Polish adaptations of French operas as musically less attractive and did not set his hand to creating such works until the first decade of the nineteenth century. Not even news about the enormous success of Paris's best actress-singer, Warsaw's former soprano Saint-Huberty, evoked renewed broad interest in original *opéra-comique*. Following Montbrun's interrupted season, there were no further plans to establish a French company at the public theatre. Having been ousted from the public stage, French comedies and *opéra-comique* continued to flourish at magnate residencies and the king's private theatre. In March 1779, members of the *théâtre de société* concentrated around Magdalena Agnieszka Sapieżyna entertained themselves with *La colonie*, an adaptation of *L'isola d'amore* with music by Sacchini (previously produced by Montbrun). The same month alone saw noble amateurs acting and singing on a private stage in *Les trois fermiers* (Monvel – Dèzede).[287] In these circumstances, the actor-singers prematurely released from Montbrun's troupe found employment at the theatre of Kazimierz Poniatowski until January 1779.

The emergence of Polish opera during Montbrun's enterprise – incidentally, abounding in *opéra-comique* premieres – did not exert a direct negative effect on the French-language spectacles. It occurred too late to have decisively reoriented the taste of the audience. At the same time, however, the disparities between theatrical preferences grew along with the Polish theatre's coming into

---

[285] 'La musique de cet opéra, faite par un Italien, est superbe et si ces diables de français avayent voulu brailler un peu moins, tout spectacle en générale aurait été charmant'. Kazimierz Ustrzycki to Stanisław Potocki, quoted in Wierzbicka-Michalska, *Sześć studiów*, p. 234.

[286] 'Nie jest ona najlepsza dla uszu warszawskich, bo ma wiele krzykliwej francuszczyzny'. Feliks Oraczewski to Stanisław August Poniatowski, 30 January 1792, quoted in Zawadzki, 'Teatr we wspomnieniach', pp. 655–7.

[287] A handwritten newspaper from Warsaw, 4 March 1779 and 18 March 1779, in Jackl, 'Teatr stanisławowski', 40–1; Czartoryski, *Memoirs of Prince*, vol. 1, p. 27.

its own. According to Bogusławski, the national troupe had 'much approached perfection' in spoken comedy by 1778.[288] Ogiński's description of the Polish actors as no less skilful than the French ones corroborates this opinion.[289] It was not without importance that the Polish theatre had been absorbing French spoken and sung repertoires. In a sense, Polish-language opera substituted for absent *opéra-comique* by means of adaptations of the French works that had already been familiar to the Warsaw operagoers. The fall of a French theatre outside France, that epitome of universal Enlightenment ideals, was imposed by general demand as well as compensated by accelerating advancement of domestic operatic creativity.

---

[288] Bogusławski, *Dzieje Teatru Narodowego*, p. 18.
[289] Wierzbicka-Michalska, 'Scena', p. 802.

Bibliography

Archives

Cracow, Biblioteka Czartoryskich (BCz), 965; 2037.

Cracow, Biblioteka Jagiellońska (BJ), 6117 IV; 6118 II.

Kórnik, Biblioteka Kórnicka (BK), 1328.

Warsaw, Archiwum Główne Akt Dawnych (AGAD), Archiwum Ghigiottiego (AG), 451.

Warsaw, Archiwum Główne Akt Dawnych (AGAD), Archiwum Ks. Józefa Poniatowskiego i Marii Teresy z Poniatowskich Tyszkiewiczowej (AJP), 292; 444; 445.

Warsaw, Archiwum Główne Akt Dawnych (AGAD), Archiwum Rodzinne Poniatowskich (ARP), 415.

Warsaw, Archiwum Główne Akt Dawnych (AGAD), Archiwum Tyzenhauzów (AT), F 23.

Warsaw, Archiwum Główne Akt Dawnych (AGAD), Księgi Miejskie Warszawa – Ekonomiczne (KMWE), 859.

Warsaw, Archiwum Główne Akt Dawnych (AGAD), Archiwum Zamoyskich (AZ), 3063.

Warsaw, Biblioteka Narodowa (BN), Collection of playbills.

Warsaw, Instytut Sztuki Polskiej Akademii Nauk (ISPAN), Archiwum Mieczysława Rulikowskiego (AMR), 1067 59 (1); 1067 60 (2); 1067 63 (1).

Warsaw, Muzeum Teatralne (MT), Collection of playbills.

Published Archival Materials

Bernacki, Ludwik, *Teatr, dramat i muzyka za Stanisława Augusta*, 2 vols (Lviv: Wydawnictwo Zakładu Narodowego Imienia Ossolińskich, 1925).

Jackl, Jerzy, 'Litteraria' in Jan Kott (ed.), *Teatr Narodowy, 1765–1794* (Warsaw: Państwowy Instytut Wydawniczy, 1967), pp. 331–431.

'Teatr stanisławowski w prasie współczesnej polskiej i obcej: Aneksy', *Pamiętnik Teatralny* 16, no. 1 (1967), 22–89.

'Teatr i życie teatralne w gazetach i gazetkach pisanych (1763–1794)' in Jan Kott (ed.), *Teatr Narodowy, 1765–1794* (Warsaw: Państwowy Instytut Wydawniczy, 1967), pp. 433–615.

Kaleta, Roman, 'Wzmianki o życiu teatralnym Warszawy w korespondencji Marianny z Kątskich Potockiej (1765–1766)', *Pamiętnik Teatralny* 15, nos. 1–4 (1966), 146–66.

Klimowicz, Mieczysław, *Teatr Narodowy, 1765–1766: Raporty szpiega; Podpatrzył i opisał Jan Heine agent Franciszka Xawerego królewicza polskiego księcia regenta saskiego* (Warsaw: Instytut Sztuki PAN, 1962).

Pawłowiczowa, Janina, 'Teoria i krytyka' in Jan Kott (ed.), *Teatr Narodowy, 1765–1794* (Warsaw: Państwowy Instytut Wydawniczy, 1967), pp. 69–330.

Rulikowski, Mieczysław, *Warszawski teatr Sułkowskich: Dokumenty z lat 1774–1785*, ed. by Barbara Król (Wrocław: Zakład Narodowy Imienia Ossolińskich, 1957).

Wierzbicka, Karyna, *Źródła do historii teatru warszawskiego od roku 1762 do roku 1833*, 2 vols (Wrocław: Wydawnictwo Zakładu Narodowego Imienia Ossolińskich, 1951).

Wierzbicka-Michalska, Karyna, 'Scena 1765–1795' in Jan Kott (ed.), *Teatr Narodowy, 1765–1794* (Warsaw: Państwowy Instytut Wydawniczy, 1967), pp. 743–841.

Zawadzki, 'Teatr we wspomnieniach i listach' in Jan Kott (ed.), *Teatr Narodowy, 1765–1794* (Warsaw: Państwowy Instytut Wydawniczy, 1967), pp. 617–739.

Primary Sources

Books and Articles

Albertrandi, Jan Chrzciciel, 'Przedmowa', *Zabawy przyjemne i pożyteczne* 1, no. 1 (1770), i–xi.

Baudouin, Jan, *Utwory dramatyczne: Wybór*, ed. by Maria Wielanier (Warsaw: Państwowy Instytut Wydawniczy, 1966).

Biester, Johann Erich, 'Einige Briefe über Polen: Geschrieben im Sommer 1791', *Berlinische Monatschrift* 19 (1792), 545–603.

Bogusławski, Wojciech, *Dzieje Teatru Narodowego na trzy części podzielone oraz wiadomość o życiu sławnych artystów* (Warsaw: Glücksberg, 1820).

'Uwagi nad operą *Jozef w Egiptcie*' in *Dzieła dramatyczne*, vol. 1, pp. 357–64 (Warsaw: Glücksberg, 1820).

'Uwagi nad operą *Sługa panią*' in *Dzieła dramatyczne*, vol. 10, pp. 307–8 (Warsaw: Glücksberg, 1823.

[Bohomolec, Franciszek], 'Mci Panie Monitor', *Monitor*, no. 88 (2 November 1768), 800–7.

Casanova, Giacomo, *History of My Life*, trans. by Willard R. Trask, vol. 10 (Baltimore: The Johns Hopkins University Press, 1997).

Coxe, William, *Travels into Poland, Russia, Sweden, and Denmark*, vol. 2 (London: T. Cadell, 1784).

[Czacki, Michał], *Wspomnienie z roku 1788 po 1792* (Poznań: Żupański, 1862).

Czartoryski, Adam Jerzy, *Memoirs of Prince Adam Czartoryski and His Correspondence with Alexander I*, ed. by Adam Gielgud, vol. 1 (London: Remington, 1888).

[Czartoryski, Adam Kazimierz], preface to *Panna na wydaniu*, 2nd ed. (Warsaw: Gröll, 1779), pp. 9–84.

[Edgcumbe, Richard], *Musical Reminiscences of an Old Amateur Chiefly Respecting the Italian Opera in England for Fifty Years, from 1773 to 1823*, 2nd ed. (London: Clarke, 1827).

Engeström, Lars von, *Pamiętniki Wawrzyńca hr. Engeströma*, trans. by Józef Ignacy Kraszewski (Poznań: Żupański, 1875).

[Essen, August Franz], 'Correspondence sur les affaires politiques du royaume de Pologne, de l'annee 1763 jusqu'a 1766', *Magazin für die neue Historie und Geographie* 13 (1779), 1–76.

Geoffrin, Marie Thérèse and Stanisław August Poniatowski, *Correspondance inédite du roi Stanislas-Auguste Poniatowski et de Madame Geoffrin (1764–1777)*, ed. by Charles de Mouÿ (Paris: Plon, 1875).

Golański, Filip Neriusz, *O wymowie i poezyi*, 2nd ed. (Vilnius: Scholarum Piarum, 1788).

Heyking, Karl Heinrich, *Aus Polens und Kurlands letzten Tagen*, ed. by Alfons Heyking (Berlin: Räder, 1897).

Jakubowski, Wojciech, *Listy Wojciecha Jakubowskiego do Jana Klemensa Branickiego W. Hetmana Koronnego z lat 1758–1771*, ed. by Julian Bartoszewicz (Warsaw: Świdzińscy, 1882).

Jezierski, Franciszek Salezy, *Niektóre wyrazy porządkiem abecadła zebrane y stosownemi do rzeczy uwagami objaśnione* (Warsaw: Gröll, 1792).

[Krasicki, Ignacy], *Monitor*, no. 27 (1765), 204–11.

Monitor, no. 50 (1765), 386–92.

Magier, Antoni, *Estetyka miasta stołecznego Warszawy*, ed. by Hanna Szwankowska (Wrocław: Zakład Narodowy Imienia Ossolińskich, 1963).

[Michniewski, Antoni Tadeusz], 'Mości Panie Monitor', *Monitor*, no. 53 (2 July 1774), 121–127.

[Mitzler, Lorenz Christoph], *Brief eines Gelehrten aus Wilna an einen bekannten Schriftsteller in Warschau die Polnischen Schaubühnen betreffend* (Warsaw: Mitzler, 1775).

Dritter Brief eines Warschauer Schriftstellers an den Herrn Lorenz von Lehrlieben in Wilna (Warsaw: Mitzler, 1775).

Fünfter und letzter Brief eines Warschauer Schriftstellers an den Herrn Lorenz von Lehrlieben in Wilna (Warsaw: Mitzler, 1776).

'O dobrym porządku towarzystwa, a w szczególności o rozrywkach', *Monitor*, no. 71 (3 September 1774), 500–7.

Vierter Brief eines Gelehrten aus Wilna an einen bekannten Schriftsteller in Warschau die Warschauer Schaubühne betreffend (Warsaw: Mitzler, 1776).

Zweyter Brief eines Gelehrten aus Wilna an einen bekannten Schriftsteller in Warschau, die Warschauer Schaubühne betreffend (Warsaw: Mitzler, 1775).

Moszyński, August, *Dziennik podróży do Francji i Włoch Augusta Moszyńskiego architekta JKM Stanisława Augusta Poniatowskiego, 1784–1786*, ed. by Bożena Zboińska-Daszyńska (Cracow: Wydawnictwo Literackie, 1970).

[Müller, Wilhelm Christian], *Beyträge zur Lebensgeschichte des Schauspieldirektor Abbt's* (Frankfurt: N.p., 1784).

Niemcewicz, Julian Ursyn, *Pamiętniki czasów moich*, ed. by Jan Dihm, 2 vols (Warsaw: Państwowy Instytut Wydawniczy, 1957).

[Potocki, Ignacy], *Listy polskie pisane w roku 1785*, vol. 1 (Lviv: Wit, n.d.).

[Schulz], Friedrich, *Reise eines Liefländers von Riga nach Warschau, durch Südpreußen, über Breslau, . . . nach Botzen in Tyrol*, 4 vols (Berlin: n.p., 1795).

Sierakowski, Wacław, *Sztuka muzyki dla młodzieży kraiowey*, vol.1 (Cracow: Drukarnia Szkoły Głowney Koronney, 1795–96).

[Świtkowski, Piotr], 'Charakter Włochów', *Magazyn Warszawski* 2, no. 1 (1785), 73–85.

'Rozrywki Angielczyków', *Pamiętnik Historyczno-Polityczny* 5, no. 12 (1786), 176–220.

[Wittenberg, Albrecht], *Briefe über die Ackermannsche und Hamonsche Schauspieler Gesellschaft zu Hamburg* (Berlin: N.p., 1776).

Wraxall, N. William, *Memoirs of the Courts of Berlin, Dresden, Warsaw, and Vienna in the Years 1777, 1778, and 1779*, 2 vols., 2nd ed. (London: Cadell, 1800).

Journals, Newspapers, and Almanacs

Annonces et Avis Divers de Varsovie (Warsaw, 1781–84)

Briefe eines Gelehrten aus Wilna (Warsaw, 1775–76)

Gazeta Warszawska (Warsaw, 1774–93)

Indice de' Teatrali Spettacoli (Milan, 1764–1800)

Journal Littéraire de Varsovie (Warsaw, 1777–78)

Litteratur- und Theater Zeitung (Berlin, 1778–84)

Monitor (Warsaw, 1765–85)

Theater-Journal für Deutschland (Gotha, 1778–84)

Theater-Kalender auf das Jahr . . . (Gotha, 1775–1800)

Librettos

Il dissoluto punito o sia Il D. Giovanni (Warsaw: Dufour, 1789)

Nędza uszczęśliwiona (Warsaw: Dufour, 1778).

Prostota cnotliwa (Warsaw: Drukarnia Nadworna J.K. Mci, 1779).

Zenobia di Palmira (Warsaw: Dufour, 1791)

Zośka czyli wiejskie zaloty, 2nd ed. (Warsaw: Dufour, 1784).

Secondary Sources

Adorno, Theodor W., 'Bourgeois Opera' in *Sound Figures* (translated by Rodney Livingstone) (Stanford: Stanford University Press, 1999), pp. 15–28.

Bauman, Thomas, *North German Opera in the Age of Goethe* (Cambridge: Cambridge University Press, 1985).

Beaurepaire, Pierre-Yves and Charlotta Wolff, 'Introduction' in Pierre-Yves Beaurepaire, Philippe Bourdin, and Charlotta Wolff (eds.), *Moving Scenes: The Circulation of Music and Theatre in Europe, 1700–1815* (Oxford: Voltaire Foundation, 2018), pp. 1–6.

Beaurepaire, Pierre-Yves, Philippe Bourdin, and Charlotta Wolff (eds.), *Moving Scenes: The Circulation of Music and Theatre in Europe, 1700–1815* (Oxford: Voltaire Foundation, 2018).

Berdecka, Anna and Irena Turnau, *Życie codzienne w Warszawie okresu Oświecenia* (Warsaw: Państwowy Instytut Wydawniczy, 1969).

Bilton, Peter, George Bisztray, Barbara Day, et al. (eds.), *National Theatre in Northern and Eastern Europe, 1746–1900* (Cambridge: Cambridge University Press, 1991).

Blanning, Timothy Charles William, *The Culture of Power and the Power of Culture: Old Regime Europe, 1660–1789* (Oxford: Oxford University Press, 2002).

Bogucka, Maria, 'Between Capital, Residential Town and Metropolis: The Development of Warsaw in the Sixteenth to Eighteenth Centuries' in Peter Clark and Bernard Lepetit (eds.), *Capital Cities and Their Hinterlands in Early Modern Europe* (Aldershot: Scolar Press, 1996), pp. 198–216.

Henryk Samsonowicz, *Dzieje miast i mieszczaństwa w Polsce przedrozbiorowej* (Wrocław: Zakład Narodowy Imienia Ossolińskich, 1986).

Maria I. Kwiatkowska, Marek Kwiatkowski, Władysław Tomkiewicz, and Andrzej Zahorski, *Dzieje Warszawy, tom II: Warszawa w latach 1526–1795* ed. Stefan Kieniewicz (Warsaw: Państwowe Wydawnictwo Naukowe, 1984).

Brown, Bruce Alan, *Gluck and the French Theatre in Vienna* (Oxford: Clarendon Press, 1991).

'*Lo specchio francese*: Viennese Opera Buffa and the Legacy of French Theatre' in Mary Hunter and James Webster (eds.), *Opera Buffa in Mozart's Vienna* (Cambridge: Cambridge University Press, 1997), pp. 50–81.

Bucciarelli, Melania, Norbert Dubowy, and Reinhard Strohm (eds.), *Italian Opera in Central Europe, Volume 1: Institutions and Ceremonies* (Berlin: Berliner Wissenschafts-Verlag, 2006).

Butterwick, Richard, *Poland's Last King and English Culture: Stanisław August Poniatowski (1732–1798)* (Oxford: Clarendon Press, 1998).

'Stanisław August Poniatowski – patriota oświecony i kosmopolityczny', *Wiek Oświecenia* 15 (1999), 41–55.

Castelvecchi, Stefano, *Sentimental Opera: Questions of Genre in the Age of Bourgeois Drama* (Cambridge: Cambridge University Press, 2013).

Charlton, David, *Grétry and the Growth of Opéra-Comique* (Cambridge: Cambridge University Press, 1986).

Popular Opera in Eighteenth-Century France: Music and Entertainment before the Revolution (Cambridge: Cambridge University Press, 2022).

Ciesielski, Zenon (ed.), *Skandynawia w oczach Polaków: Antologia* (Gdańsk: Wydawnictwo Morskie, 1974).

Dahlhaus, Carl, 'The Eighteenth Century as a Music-Historical Epoch' (Translated by Ernest Harriss), *College Music Symposium* 26 (1986), 1–6.

Davies, Norman, *Heart of Europe: A Short History of Poland* (Oxford: Clarendon Press, 1984).

Doe, Julia, *The Comedians of the King*: Opéra Comique *and the Bourbon Monarchy on the Eve of Revolution* (Chicago: The University of Chicago Press, 2021).

Dubowy, Norbert, 'Introduction' in Melania Bucciarelli, Norbert Dubowy, and Reinhard Strohm (eds.), *Italian Opera in Central Europe, Volume 1: Institutions and Ceremonies* (Berlin: Berliner Wissenschafts-Verlag, 2006), pp. 1–7.

Corinna Herr and Alina Żórawska-Witkowska (eds.), *Italian Opera in Central Europe, 1614–1780, Volume 3: Opera Subjects and European Relationships* (Berlin: Berliner Wissenschafts-Verlag, 2007).

Emery, Ted, *Goldoni as Librettist: Theatrical Reform and the* drammi giocosi per musica (New York: Peter Lang, 1991).

Glatthorn, Austin, *Music Theatre and the Holy Roman Empire: The German Musical Stage at the Turn of the Nineteenth Century* (Cambridge: Cambridge University Press, 2022).

Goehring, Edmund J., 'The Sentimental Muse of Opera Buffa' in Mary Hunter and James Webster (eds.), *Opera Buffa in Mozart's Vienna* (Cambridge: Cambridge University Press, 1997), pp. 115–45.

Gordon, Felicia and P. N. Furbank, *Marie Madeleine Jodin, 1741–1790: Actress*, Philosophe *and Feminist* (London: Routledge, 2016).

Got, Jerzy, *Das österreichische Theater in Krakau im 18. und 19. Jahrhundert* (Vienna: Verlag der Österreichische Akademie der Wissenschaften, 1984).

Na wyspie Guaxary: Wojciech Bogusławski i teatr lwowski, 1789–1799 (Cracow: Wydawnictwo Literackie, 1971).

Grochulska, Barbara, 'Miejsce Warszawy w Polsce stanisławowskiej' in Marian Marek Drozdowski (ed.), *Warszawa w dziejach Polski: Materiały sesji naukowej zorganizowanej przez Obywatelski Komitet Obchodów 400-lecia Stołeczności Warszawy, Polską Akademię Nauk i Towarzystwo Miłośników Historii, 15–16 maja 1996 roku, Zamek Królewski w Warszawie* (Warsaw: Wydawnictwo Instytutu Historii PAN, 1998), pp. 105–19.

Grześkowiak-Krwawicz, Anna, *Queen Liberty: The Concept of Freedom in the Polish-Lithuanian Commonwealth* (Translated by Daniel J. Sax) (Leiden: Brill, 2012).

Guzy-Pasiak, Jolanta and Aneta Markuszewska (eds.), *Music Migration in the Early Modern Age: Centres and Peripheries – People, Works, Styles, Paths of Dissemination and Influence* (Warsaw: Liber Pro Arte, 2016).

Habermas, Jürgen, *The Structural Transformation of the Public Sphere: An Inquiry into a Category of Bourgeois Society* (Translated by Thomas Burger) (Cambridge, MA: The MIT Press, 1989).

Hass, Ludwik, *Sekta farmazonii warszawskiej. Pierwsze stulecie wolnomularstwa w Warszawie (1721–1821)* (Warsaw: Państwowy Instytut Wydawniczy, 1980).

Heartz, Daniel, *From Garrick to Gluck: Essays on Opera in the Age of Enlightenment*, ed. by John A. Rice (Hillsdale: Pendragon Press, 2004).

Music in European Capitals: The Galant Style, 1720–1780 (New York: Norton, 2003).

Herr, Corinna, Herbert Seifert, Andrea Sommer-Mathis and Reinhard Strohm (eds.), *Italian Opera in Central Europe, Vol 2: Italianità: Image and Practice* (Berlin: Berliner Wissenschafts-Verlag, 2008).

Hoven, Lena van der, Kordula Knaus and Andrea Zedler, *Die Opera Buffa in Europa: Verbreitungs- und Transformationsprozesse einer neuen Gattung (1740–1765)* (Bielefeld: Transcript, 2023).

Hunter, Mary, 'Nobility in Mozart's Operas' in Rachel Cowgill, David Cooper, and Clive Brown (eds.) *Art and Ideology in European Opera: Essays in Honour of Julian Rushton* (Woodbridge: The Boydell Press, 2010), pp. 176–93.

The Culture of Opera Buffa in Mozart's Vienna: A Poetics of Entertainment (Princeton: Princeton University Press, 1999).

Jackl, Jerzy, 'Król czy Stackelberg? W sprawie restytucji Teatru Narodowego w 1774', *Pamiętnik Teatralny* 18, nos. 1–2 (1969), 65–109.

Janowski, Maciej, *Narodziny Inteligencji, 1750–1831* (Warsaw: Neriton, 2008).

Katalinić, Vjera (ed.), *Music Migrations in the Early Modern Age: People, Markets, Patterns and Styles* (Zagreb: Croatian Musicological Society, 2016).

Klimowicz, Mieczysław, *Początki teatru stanisławowskiego (1765–1773)* (Warsaw: Państwowy Instytut Wydawniczy, 1965).

'Repertuar teatru warszawskiego w latach 1765–1767', *Pamiętnik Teatralny* 11, no. 2 (1962), 237–61.

Kochanowicz, Jacek, *Backwardness and Modernization: Poland and Eastern Europe in the 16th–20th Centuries* (Aldershot: Ashgate Variorum, 2006).

Korneeva, Tatiana, 'Introduction: Italian Theatre Reverberated' in Tatiana Korneeva (ed.), *Mapping Artistic Networks: Eighteenth-Century Italian Theatre and Opera Across Europe* (Turnhout: Brepols, 2021), pp. 11–21.

Korneeva, Tatiana (ed.), *Mapping Artistic Networks: Eighteenth-Century Italian Theatre and Opera across Europe* (Turnhout: Brepols, 2021).

Kostkiewiczowa, Teresa, *Polski wiek świateł: Obszary swoistości* (Wrocław: Wydawnictwo Uniwersytetu Wrocławskiego, 2002).

Kott, Jan and Stanisław Lorentz (eds.), *Warszawa wieku Oświecenia* (Warsaw: Państwowy Instytut Wydawniczy, 1954).

Król-Kaczorowska, Barbara, *Teatry Warszawy: Budynki i sale w latach 1748–1975* (Warsaw: Państwowy Instytut Wydawniczy, 1986).

Link, Dorothea, *The National Court Theatre in Mozart's Vienna: Sources and Documents, 1783–1792* (Oxford: Clarendon Press, 1998).

Lukowski, Jerzy, *Disorderly Liberty: The Political Culture of the Polish-Lithuanian Commonwealth in the Eighteenth Century* (London: Continuum, 2010).

Maciejewski, Janusz, 'Geneza i charakter ideologii republikantów, 1767–1775', *Archiwum Historii Filozofii i Myśli Społecznej* 17 (1971), 45–84.

Markovits, Rahul, [translated by Jane Marie Todd] *Staging Civilization: A Transnational History of French Theater in Eighteenth-Century Europe* (Charlottesville: University of Virginia Press, 2021).

Meer, Jan IJ. van der, *Literary Activities and Attitudes in the Stanislavian Age in Poland (1764–1795): A Social System?* (Amsterdam: Rodopi, 2002).

Mele, Flora, 'The Adaptation of French Performance as Shown in Favart's Correspondence' in Pierre-Yves Beaurepaire, Philippe Bourdin, and Charlotta Wolff (eds.), *Moving Scenes: The Circulation of Music and Theatre in Europe, 1700–1815* (Oxford: Voltaire Foundation, 2018), pp. 127–42.

Mongrédien, Jean, '*Les Mystères d'Isis* (1801) and Reflections on Mozart from the Parisian Press at the Beginning of the Nineteenth Century' in Allan W. Atlas (ed.), *Music in the Classic Period: Essays in Honor of Barry S. Brook* (New York: Pendragon Press, 1985), pp. 195–211.

Murphy, Curtis G., *From Citizens to Subjects: City, State, & the Enlightenment in Poland, Ukraine, & Belarus* (Pittsburgh: University of Pittsburgh Press, 2018).

Münchheimer, Adam, 'Don Juan w Warszawie', *Echo Muzyczne i Teatralne*, no. 20 (1884), 216.

Nedbal, Martin, *Morality and Viennese Opera in the Age of Mozart and Beethoven* (London: Routledge, 2016).

Nieden, Gesa zur and Berthold Over (eds.), *Musicians' Mobilities and Music Migrations in Early Modern Europe: Biographical Patterns and Cultural Exchanges* (Bielefeld: Transcript, 2016).

Niubo, Marc, 'The Italian Opera in Prague in the Eighteenth Century: Networks, Strategies, Repertoires' in Tatiana Korneeva (ed.), *Mapping Artistic Networks: Eighteenth-Century Italian Theatre and Opera across Europe* (Turnhout: Brepols, 2021), pp. 41–52.

Olkusz, Piotr, 'Poniatowski's National Theatre: The Idea and Institution of Enlightenment' in Katarzyna Fazan, Michal Kobialka, and Bryce Lease (eds.), *A History of Polish Theatre* (Cambridge: Cambridge University Press, 2022), pp. 68–82.

Ozimek, Stanisław, *Udział 'Monitora' w kształtowaniu Teatru Narodowego (1765–1785)* (Wrocław: Zakład Narodowy Imienia Ossolińskich, 1957).

Parkitna, Anna, 'Pursuing Enlightenment Delights: Processes and Paths of Italian Operatic Migrations to Warsaw, 1765–93' in Tatiana Korneeva (ed.), *Mapping Artistic Networks: Eighteenth-Century Italian Theatre and Opera across Europe* (Turnhout: Brepols, 2021), pp. 53–63.

Parkitny, Maciej, *Nowoczesność oświecenia: Studia o literaturze i kulturze polskiej drugiej połowy XVIII wieku* (Poznań: Wydawnictwo Naukowe UAM, 2018).

Pelc, Janusz, *Barok – epoka przeciwieństw* (Warsaw: Czytelnik, 1993).

Pendle, Karin, 'Opéra-Comique as Literature: The Spread of French Styles in Europe, ca. 1760 to the Revolution' in Philippe Vendrix (ed.), *Grétry et l'Europe de l'opéra-comique* (Liège: Mardaga, 1992), pp. 229–50.

Piperno, Franco, 'Opera Production to 1780' in Lorenzo Bianconi and Giorgio Pestelli (eds.), [translated by Lydia G. Cochrane] *Opera Production and Its Resources* (Chicago: Chicago University Press, 1998), pp. 1–79.

Piperno, Franco, 'State and Market, Production and Style: An Interdisciplinary Approach to Eighteenth-Century Italian Opera History' in Victoria Johnson, Jane F. Fulcher, and Thomas Ertman (eds.), *Opera and Society in Italy and France from Monteverdi to Bourdieu* (Cambridge: Cambridge University Press, 2007), pp. 138–59.

Porfirieva, Anna and Marina Ritzarev, 'The Italian Diaspora in Eighteenth-Century Russia' in Reinhard Strohm (ed.), *The Eighteenth-Century Diaspora of Italian Music and Musicians* (Turnhout: Brepols, 2001), pp. 211–53.

Raszewski, Zbigniew, *Staroświecczyzna i postęp czasu: O teatrze polskim (1765–1865)* (Warsaw: Państwowy Instytut Wydawniczy, 1963).

Teatr na placu Krasińskich (Warsaw: Wydawnictwo Krąg, 1995).

Trudny rebus: Studia i szkice z historii teatru (Wrocław: Wiedza o Kulturze, 1990).

Ratajczakowa, Dobrochna, *Komedia oświeconych, 1752–1795* (Warsaw: Wydawnictwo Naukowe PWN, 1993).

Reiss, Józef, 'Do dziejów teatru za Stanisława Augusta w Polsce', *Pamiętnik Literacki* 26, no. 1–4 (1929), 606–8.

Rice, John, 'Antonio Baglioni, Mozart's First Don Ottavio and Tito, in Italy and Prague' in Milada Jonášová and Tomislav Volek (eds.), *Böhmische Aspekte des Lebens und des Werkes von W. A. Mozart: Bericht über die Prager internationale Konferenz, 27– 28. Oktober 2006* (Prague: Ethnologische Institut für Ethnologie der Akademie der Wissenschaften der Tschechischer Republik, 2011), pp. 24–38.

Antonio Salieri and Viennese Opera (Chicago: The University of Chicago Press, 1998).

'Leopold II, Mozart, and the Return to a Golden Age' in Thomas Bauman and Marita Petzoldt McClymonds (eds.), *Opera and the Enlightenment* (Cambridge: Cambridge University Press, 1995), pp. 271–96.

Mozart on the Stage (Cambridge: Cambridge University Press, 2008).

'Sense, Sensibility, and Opera Seria: An Epistolary Debate', *Studi Musicali* 15 (1986), 101–38.

Rosselli, John, *Singers of Italian Opera: The History of a Profession* (Cambridge: Cambridge University Press, 1992).

The Opera Industry in Italy from Cimarosa to Verdi: The Role of the Impresario (Cambridge: Cambridge University Press, 1984).

Roszak, Stanisław, *Środowisko intelektualne i artystyczne Warszawy w połowie XVIII wieku: Między kulturą sarmatyzmu i oświecenia* (Toruń: Wydawnictwo Adam Marszałek, 1998).

Ryszka-Komarnicka, Anna, 'From Venice to Warsaw: *Zenobia di Palmira* by Sertor and Anfossi Performed by Guardasoni's Troupe (1791)' in Kathryn L. Libin (ed.), *Mozart in Prague: Essays on Performance, Patronage, Sources, and Reception; Proceedings of the Mozart Society of America / Society for Eighteenth-Century Music Conference in Prague, 9–13 June 2009* (Prague: Mozart Society of America, 2016), pp. 295–310.

Salmonowicz, Stanisław, *Polacy i Niemcy wobec siebie: Postawy – Opinie – Stereotypy (1697–1815); Próba zarysu* (Olsztyn: Ośrodek Badań Naukowych im. Wojciecha Kętrzyńskiego, 1993).

Scuderi, Cristina and Ingeborg Zechner (eds.), *Opera as Institution: Networks and Professions (1730–1917)* (Vienna: LIT Verlag, 2019).

Sennett, Richard, *The Fall of Public Man* (Cambridge: Cambridge University Press, 1977).

Snopek, Jerzy, *Objawienie i Oświecenie: Z dziejów libertynizmu w Polsce* (Wrocław: Zakład Narodowy Imienia Ossolińskich, 1986).

Strohm, Reinhard (ed.), *The Eighteenth-Century Diaspora of Italian Music and Musicians* (Turnhout: Brepols, 2001).

'The Wanderings of Music through Space and Time' in Jolanta Guzy-Pasiak and Aneta Markuszewska (eds.), *Music Migration in the Early Modern Age: Centres and Peripheries – People, Works, Styles, Paths of Dissemination and Influence* (Warsaw: Liber Pro Arte, 2016), pp. 17–32.

Targosz-Kretowa, Karolina, *Teatr dworski Władysława IV (1635–1648)* (Cracow: Wydawnictwo Literackie, 1965).

Tazbir, Janusz, *Kultura szlachecka w Polsce: Rozkwit – Upadek – Relikty* (Warsaw: Wiedza Powszechna, 1978).

Walicki, Andrzej, *The Enlightenment and the Birth of Modern Nationhood: Polish Political Thought from Noble Republicanism to Tadeusz Kościuszko* (Translated by Emma Harris) (Notre Dame: University of Notre Dame Press, 1989).

Weber, William, 'Cosmopolitan, National, and Regional Identities in Eighteenth-Century European Musical Life' in Jane F. Fulcher (ed.), *The Oxford Handbook of the New Cultural History of Music* (Oxford: Oxford University Press, 2011), pp. 209–27.

'Did People Listen in the 18th Century?', *Early Music* 25, no. 4 (1997), pp. 678–91.

Wiel, Taddeo, *I teatri musicali veneziani del settecento: Catalogo delle opere in musica rappresentate nel secolo XVIII in Venezia (1701–1800)* (Venice: Visentini, 1897).

Wierzbicka, Karyna, *Życie teatralne w Warszawie za Stanisława Augusta* (Warsaw: Towarzystwo Miłośników Historii, 1949).

Wierzbicka-Michalska, Karyna, *Aktorzy cudzoziemscy w Warszawie w XVIII wieku* (Wrocław: Zakład Narodowy Imienia Ossolińskich, 1975).

Sześć studiów o teatrze stanisławowskim (Wrocław: Zakład Narodowy Imienia Ossolińskich, 1967).

Williams, Simon, *German Actors of the Eighteenth and Nineteenth Centuries: Idealism, Romanticism, and Realism* (Wesport: Greenwood Press, 1985).

Wolff, Charlotta, 'Lyrical Diplomacy: Count Gustav Philip Creutz (1731–1785) and the Opera' in Pierre-Yves Beaurepaire, Philippe Bourdin, and Charlotta Wolff (eds.), *Moving Scenes: The Circulation of Music and Theatre in Europe, 1700–1815* (Oxford: Voltaire Foundation, 2018), pp. 143–56.

Woodfield, Ian, *Performing Operas for Mozart: Impresarios, Singers and Troupes* (Cambridge: Cambridge University Press, 2012).

The Vienna Don Giovanni (Woodbridge: The Boydell Press, 2010).

Woźnowski, Wacław, *Pamflet obyczajowy w czasach Stanisława Augusta* (Wrocław: Zakład Narodowy Imienia Ossolińskich, 1973).

Zajas, Krzysztof, 'The Ambiguous Republic' in Katarzyna Fazan, Michal Kobialka, and Bryce Lease (eds.), *A History of Polish Theatre* (Cambridge: Cambridge University Press, 2022), pp. 16–26.

Zamoyski, Adam, *The Last King of Poland* (London: Weidenfeld and Nicolson, 1997).

Zechmeister, Gustav, *Die Wiener Theater nächst der Burg und nächst dem Kärntnerthor von 1747 bis 1776* (Vienna: Böhlau, 1971).

Zieliński, Marek Grzegorz, *Cudzoziemcy w życiu codziennym Rzeczypospolitej doby stanisławowskiej* (Bydgoszcz: Wydawnictwo Akademii Bydgoskiej, 2004).

Żórawska-Witkowska, Alina, 'Eighteenth-Century Warsaw: Periphery, Keystone, (and) Centre of European Musical Culture' in Jolanta Guzy-Pasiak and Aneta Markuszewska (eds.), *Music Migration in the Early Modern Age: Centres and Peripheries – People, Works, Styles, Paths of Dissemination and Influence* (Warsaw: Liber Pro Arte, 2016), pp. 33–52.

Muzyka na dworze i w teatrze Stanisława Augusta (Warsaw: Zamek Królewski w Warszawie, 1995).

'Parodies of *Dramma per Musica* at the Warsaw Theatre of August III' in Norbert Dubowy, Corinna Herr and Alina Żórawska-Witkowska (eds.), *Italian Opera in Central Europe, 1614–1780, Volume 3: Opera Subjects and European Relationships* (Berlin: Berliner Wissenschafts-Verlag, 2007), pp. 125–45.

'Wokół polskiej prapremiery *Il Dissoluto punito, o sia il Don Giovanni* W. A. Mozarta (Warszawa, 14 października 1789)' in Zbigniew Skowron (ed.), *Karol Szymanowski w perspektywie kultury muzycznej przeszłości i współczesności* (Cracow: Musica Iagellonica, 2007), pp. 475–92.

Cambridge Elements ☰

Music and the City

Simon McVeigh
University of London

Simon McVeigh is Professor of Music at Goldsmiths, University of London, and President of the Royal Musical Association. His research focuses on British musical life 1700–1945; and on violin music and performance practices of the period. Books include *Concert Life in London from Mozart to Haydn* (Cambridge) and *The Italian Solo Concerto 1700–1760* (Boydell). Current work centres on London concert life around 1900: a substantial article on the London Symphony Orchestra was published in 2013 and a book exploring London's musical life in the Edwardian era is in preparation for Boydell. He is also co-investigator on the digital concert-programme initiative *InConcert*.

Abigail Wood
University of Haifa

Abigail Wood is Senior Lecturer in Ethnomusicology at the Department of Music, School of Arts, University of Haifa, and past editor of Ethnomusicology Forum. Her research focuses primarily on musical life in contemporary urban spaces, from new musical spaces among religious Jewish women, to the reflection of the Israeli-Palestinian conflict in the contested soundscapes of Jerusalem's Old City.

About the Series

Elements in Music and the City sets urban musical cultures within new global and cross-disciplinary perspectives.

The series aims to open up new ways of thinking about music in an urban context, embracing the widest diversity of music and sound in cities across the world. Breaking down boundaries between historical and contemporary, and between popular and high art, it seeks to illuminate the diverse urban environment in all its exhilarating and vivid complexity. The urban thus becomes a microcosm of a much messier, yet ultimately much richer, conception of the 'music of everyday life'.

Rigorously peer-reviewed and written by leading scholars in their fields, each Element offers authoritative and challenging approaches towards a fast-developing area of music research. Elements in Music and the City will present extended case-studies within a comparative perspective, while developing pioneering new theoretical frameworks for an emerging field.

The series is inherently cross-disciplinary and global in its perspective, as reflected in the wide-ranging multi-national advisory board. It will encourage a similar diversity of approaches, ranging from the historical and ethnomusicological to contemporary popular music and sound studies.

Written in a clear, engaging style without the need for specialist musical knowledge, *Elements in Music and the City* aims to fill the demand for easily accessible, quality texts available for teaching and research. It will be of interest not only to researchers and students in music and related arts, but also to a broad range of readers intrigued by how we might understand music and sound in its social, cultural and political contexts.